Praise for *Romps, Tots and Boffins: The Strange Language of News*

'Never has the weird language of headlines been so wittily defined.'

Libby Purves, 'Books of the Year', *The Times*

'Robert Hutton ... has set himself up as the Dr Johnson of this strange, widely read, hardly spoken, language.'

Matthew Engel, *Financial Times*

'A right romp'

Paul Dietrich, *The Metro*

'A fascinating code-breaker of the clichés, inanities and banalities which fill our newspapers. Or, if you prefer, "News Secrets Revealed Leaving Bosses Shamefaced". I'm not sure I dare write another word.'

Nick Robinson

'Finally, I understand what my fellow journalists are writing about.'

Simon Hoggart

'I'm loving a little book just out by my fellow political journalist Rob Hutton. It's ... so much more than a hilarious compendium of the ghastly cliché to which our trade is prone.'

Matthew Parris, *The Times*

'Long journey to Lib Dem Conference enlivened by Robert Hutton's journalese book, *Romps, Tots and Boffins* – hilarious, wonderful and very true – a mini classic.'

Andrew Sparrow, Guardian Politics blogger

'Very funny new book by Robert Hutton – a must-read page-turner.'

Iain Martin, former editor of the *Scotsman* and *Scotland on Sunday*

'For readers, it promises to explain what journalists really mean. And for journalists, it also provides a guide to some of the hackneyed, arcane and clichéd phrases that are probably best avoided.'

Axegrinder, *Press Gazette*

'An essential guide to finding out what you are reading about. Some people may dismiss this as a "loo book" but, actually, it's so much more.'

Ann Treneman, *The Times*

'An amusing dictionary of arcane hack-speak.'

Michael Deacon, *The Telegraph*

'The world of journalism was rocked to its foundations last night as a top newsman claimed to have discovered the secret of "journalese".'

John Rentoul, *The Independent*

WOULD THEY LIE TO YOU?

How to spin friends and manipulate people

Robert Hutton

First published 2014
by Elliott and Thompson Limited
27 John Street
London WC1N 2BX
www.eandtbooks.com

ISBN: 978-1-78396-008-8

9 8 7 6 5 4 3 2 1

A CIP catalogue record for this book is available from the British Library.

Typeset by Marie Doherty
Printed in the UK by TJ International

At one level no one trusts politicians, and politicians are obliged from time to time to conceal the full truth, to bend it and even distort it, where the interests of the bigger strategic goal demand it be done ... Without operating with some subtlety at this level, the job would be well-nigh impossible.

–Tony Blair, *A Journey*

I wasn't lying. You didn't ask the correct questions.

–Toronto Mayor Rob Ford

CONTENTS

FOREWORD
BY MATTHEW PARRIS

The best satire tells us things we know in our bones already. Holding up for scorn absurdities of which we were already aware, it illuminates them in all their preposterousness. C. Northcote Parkinson wasn't the first to observe (in his famous 1950s *Parkinson's Law*) that 'work expands to fill the time available'; mankind had long noted that the human race love to busy themselves with pointless duties. Nor was it he who found out the reasons for this. The reasons are obvious: anyone who studies human nature can guess.

No, Parkinson simply said it so much better and with such elegantly ruthless humour and such wicked examples. The deliciousness of satire is not discovery but display.

Rob Hutton has understood this. As a working political journalist he knows better than most the myriad ways in which human beings avoid telling the truth. He collects dissimulations as a lepidopterist collects butterflies, and this book is, not least, a magnificent anthology. But to the pleasures of collection he adds wit: Hutton's 'translations' from what people say to what they mean are ten-chuckles-a-minute.

Would They Lie To You? is satire, not sociology. Were the book enquiring rather than scornful, Hutton might have remarked on something rather intriguing in his collection. Amid a wealth of half-truth, euphemism and evasion, you will find very few downright lies here. Out-and-out falsehood is the exception rather than the rule.

There is a reason for this. Human beings – even bankers, lawyers and politicians – shrink from what Shakespeare called the Lie Simple. We will duck and dive and twist and turn ourselves into the most fearful knots in order to avoid telling a complete porkie. In a curious way, it's a matter of honour with us.

Many, many years ago, as a young officer in the Conservative Research Department, it was my occasional duty to put Tory politicians and would-be politicians through their paces by engaging with them in mock TV debates. Conservative Central Office would film these jousts, after which a professional tutor would take them through the recording and tell them how to improve their performances.

I was once asked to play the part of a corrupt Third-World despot, with whom a Tory hopeful did battle in our mocked-up TV studio. He came equipped with all the evidence, all the facts and figures, to prove my villainy.

But my strategy defeated him. I decided simply to lie. I did not fudge or hedge, attempt explanations, downplay the horrors or make excuses. I didn't even try to change the subject. I just flatly denied every accusation he threw at me. I said it was all made up by my enemies. 'I am the father of my people,' I kept assuring him, 'they love me. Ask them.' My poor assailant stared at me open-mouthed, and finally fell silent. He longed for a half-truth or a something-short-of-the-truth or a not-quite-the-truth to expose; but I gave him only the Lie Simple. I never gave him his 'Aha!' moment.

Study Rob Hutton's collection which follows. Note how much of the most infuriating dissimulation consists in avoidance tactics, or euphemisms, or sly ambiguities. Laugh at how often his cast of non-apologisers pretend to say sorry, or don't quite say it, or apologise for something different; but ask yourself, too, why they don't just lie: what stops them simply feigning a humiliating admission of their error?

It's because we have our pride. It's because we

cling desperately to the tortured grammar and awkward vocabulary that might be just – but only just – reconcilable with the truth. We shrink from the barefaced lie. Lying hurts, and only a psychopath feels no pain. This is why polygraph lie detectors work. Normal people sweat. The complete answer to the question 'Would they lie to you?' is 'No, not exactly *lie*'.

And it is this avoidance technique, this verbal dance, a dance with the truth that falls short of telling the truth, a dance with falsehood that falls short of the Lie Simple, that yields the rich entertainment you will find in the pages that follow.

INTRODUCTION TO THE TEXT

When my children started school, I was inevitably reminded of my own schooldays, and the strong sense I'd always had that I must have missed a day early on when someone explained what was going on. Not just where the toilets were, but all the unwritten rules that explained things like why some children got to pick the teams or how some people got to start crazes while I joined in as everyone else dropped them. This sense has never entirely left me. In adolescence, it was clear that the definition of cool behaviour had been agreed while I was out of the room. Even in adulthood, it has been hard to escape the nagging sense that I missed a vital briefing.

Which is why I was so relieved when the document that follows fell into my hands. I don't know who sent it, or why they chose me, but it arrived on my desk shortly after I'd been at a government seminar. I'd been talking about journalese, the language of news. After my usual spiel about how newspapers use journalese to cover up the gaps in their knowledge, and to make things sound more exciting than they are, I mused aloud that this wasn't so different from what companies and governments must do, except that they are trying to make things seem less exciting than they are. I think I wondered what the word for it would be, perhaps 'officialese'.

A few days later, I found a package on my desk in Westminster. Inside was this book, minus its cover, or anything else that might identify its title or author. There was no note, only a Post-It with the word 'uncommunication'.

It seemed to be some kind of textbook, a course on the uses of language by the powerful. But despite extensive searches of the archives, I can find no evidence it's ever been published. Nor can I find any evidence of any such course at an English-speaking institution. Still, this is clearly a long-standing work – one page bore the words '14th edition'. I wondered if it was a civil service manual, but while some of the content seems to be aimed at those in public life, it also covers salesmanship and even publishing, suggesting some kind of all-purpose manual for success, but one issued only to a select group. After some debate, I have decided to publish it, partly in an effort to spread knowledge more widely, but mainly in the hope that it'll sell a few copies. The text speaks for itself. Some may find it cynical or sinister, but I enjoyed its honesty. I haven't made many alterations, but where I have been able to independently verify something or add useful insight, I have inserted a footnote.

I don't know my source, so I can't say whether publication was their intention, or if my action will place them in jeopardy. If it does, I can only plead the journalists' defence: that our first duty is to the truth. I hope that if my source is forced to flee to Moscow, Venezuela or the Ecuadorian embassy, they will be able to forgive me.

Perhaps it's produced by the Illuminati, or the Freemasons, or the Bilderberg Group. I don't know. My own theory: it was given out on the first day of school, while I was still trying to find a peg to hang my coat on.

Robert Hutton
Westminster, June 2014

INTRODUCTION TO THE 14TH EDITION
Success Through Obscurity

You hold in your hands a guide that very few will ever read. Even to have been given this book means you have already distinguished yourself in some way. We have high hopes for you: past students have used our guidance to rise to the top of their chosen fields.

As you proceed through the upper echelons of society, you'll sometimes find yourself in seminars on communication, in which people in off-the-peg suits accompanied by out-of-work actors will talk about body language and 'clarity'. 'Say what you mean,' they'll tell you. Use short words, simplify your message.

We cannot emphasise too strongly how much these people miss the point.

The world can be divided into people who make complicated ideas seem simple, and people who make simple ideas complicated. Whatever area you choose, from finance to academia to the church, you'll find

WOULD THEY LIE TO YOU?

that glory, money and power flow far more freely to the complicators than the simplifiers. If that seems harsh, think of the most basic of human relationships. Anyone who's ever been on a date will recall that success rarely comes from saying what's on your mind.

This isn't a book about dating, but it is about how to succeed through obscurity. Not by lying. Lying is dangerous if you're caught, and it's quite unnecessary. You can steer a truck through the gap between a lie and the simple truth. We will now tell you how to load the truck.

The Importance of Uncommunication

Beauty is truth, and truth beauty. That may indeed be all that some people need to know, but we who follow a higher calling often deal in ugliness. From that, the world should be protected. This is why we study uncommunication, or uncomms,* as it is sometimes known.

We have explained that uncommunication isn't the same as lying. Neither is it 'waffle'. Waffle is what amateurs produce when they attempt uncomms.

---

*   Although I can find no references to 'uncommunication', the author Steven Poole came up with the term 'Unspeak' for his 2006 book on the manipulation of language. I don't know whether this is coincidence, or if he too was privy to a leak.

2

It fills the air and leaves no one in doubt that you're avoiding something. Uncommunication is a more subtle art. It sounds precise and firm to the casual listener, but it imparts no information and offers no commitments.

It is the way we smooth over life's difficult realities. It anaesthetises unpleasantness. It gets you from the point of having something that you don't quite want to say to having something you haven't quite said. It can be used to persuade people to want things they don't need or support things they don't agree with. It can give the appearance of action when there's nothing to be done.

When the ideas you'll find in this book were first set down, there were no such things as computers, and messages were sent by telegram or letter. We now live in a world of instant communication, and that calls for instant uncommunication. Indeed, this subject has become more important than ever. A well-crafted uncommunicative response can buy you the time you need to come up with a plan or distance yourself from a disaster.

This textbook covers the following areas:

Essential Uncomms · the building blocks of the subject, including the Statement of Fact and the Undenial.

Unbending Minds · how to win people to your side and sideline opponents.

Undamage Control · how to manage disasters, defend your side, and give an Unapology.

Creating an Unimpression · how to develop an undeserved reputation.

Political Uncomms · including a guide to taxation, and the only speech you'll ever need to give.

Unearning Your Keep · how to make your way in commerce.

Keeping Uncount · using statistics to your advantage.

1. ESSENTIAL UNCOMMUNICATION

We first look at the building blocks of uncommunication, the tools and techniques to which you will
find yourself returning again and again. Mastery of
these will enable you to move through life in a haze
of obscurity.

In this chapter, you will learn about:
➠ Statements of Fact
➠ Undenial
➠ Unbriefing
➠ Unanswers
➠ Pivots
➠ Unbusiness Meetings

The Statement of Fact

A basic tool in any uncommunicator's armoury is
the Statement of Fact. This is a truth placed before
your audience not to impress in its own right, but

to act as scaffolding from which the rest of your uncomms can be hung.

A good Statement of Fact is incontestable. Your goal is that no one should possibly be able to criticise you for it. Its chief effect is what it leaves unsaid.

You can see this effect in the following 2006 *Washington Post* interview with Gordon Brown, who at the time was working to shift Tony Blair out of Downing Street and replace him. The interviewer asked if he was happy with the way Blair was giving up power. Brown responded: 'It's a matter for him and the Labour Party. It's not really a matter for me at all.'

The interviewer asked about his relationship with Blair, which Blair would later compare to domestic violence, to which he replied, 'We've been working with each other for more than twenty years ... I've been chancellor while he's been prime minister for nine years, and we continue to work together.'

To see how effectively a Statement of Fact can be deployed, let's look at an area where they come into their own: when you are called upon to say something nice about someone towards whom you have absolutely no nice feelings. Perhaps you've succeeded in persuading a hated underling to quit, and now have to give a speech at their leaving party. Or maybe a lifelong enemy has finally died.

In this context, the Statement of Fact should sound like it might be admiring, without quite managing it. No one will be able to deny that you've 'paid tribute', and yet at the same time, if the subject is later shown to be a bad 'un, no one will be able to use your statement in evidence against you. It's the equivalent of writing 'Good luck!' on someone's leaving card.

Drafted correctly, Statements of Fact can fill all of the space between 'many people will be sorry to hear of the death of ...' and 'my thoughts are with their family at this difficult time'.

Here is Ed Miliband, leader of the British Labour party, following the death of the Conservative Prime Minister Margaret Thatcher in 2013:

> *She will be remembered as a unique figure. She reshaped the politics of a whole generation. She was Britain's first woman prime minister. She moved the centre ground of British politics and was a huge figure on the world stage. The Labour Party disagreed with much of what she did and she will always remain a controversial figure. But we can disagree and also greatly respect her political achievements and her personal strength.*

Note the use of 'controversial figure' here to mean

'person whose death is being marked with a party in Trafalgar Square'. In the same vein, most people can safely be described as a 'towering figure', which sounds like a compliment but might, at a push, just mean they were over 6 foot.

The Tory prime minister, David Cameron, repaid the compliment upon the death of Labour politician Tony Benn in 2014:

> *He was a magnificent writer, speaker, diarist and campaigner, with a strong record of public and political service. There was never a dull moment listening to him, even when you disagreed with everything he said.*

Given the increasing odds of much-loved TV stars turning out to have been child molesters, a Statement of Fact is also by far the safest tribute to offer any recently deceased celebrity who wasn't actually a member of your family.

Unplain Speaking

Having introduced some of the basic ideas of uncommunication, some examples may help. Note how the surface meaning is never quite wrong, but it's never quite right, either.

be honest with me · lie to me.

can you write to my office about it? · they've got a special shredder for letters in green ink.

cautiously optimistic · I think it'll either be fine, in which case I want you to thank me, or it won't, in which case I don't want you to blame me.

community · any group of people who don't get on, as in 'the theatre community'. Or a euphemism for ethnic minorities.*

could you put your request in an email? · I stopped listening about five minutes ago.

expression of concern · statement that, if accurately reflected in print, would be a string of asterisks.**

for your convenience · for our convenience, we have done something inconvenient to you. Useful in hotel signs explaining the shower will only work between 6.15 and 6.28.

humbled · proud. As in, 'I'm deeply humbled to accept this award, as I shall now demonstrate by gently boasting for the next three minutes.'

---

* This second definition may explain the 'community favourites' section that every Blockbuster Video shop used to have, in the baffling pretence that the most popular movies in the East End of Glasgow were made by Spike Lee.

** As in *The Lancet* journal's 2010 'expression of concern' after learning that one of the researchers associated with a paper on cancer it had printed might have fabricated data.

To describe people who've actually been humbled, try 'humiliated'.

I can't promise that · there is no way in Hell I'm ever going to do that.

I genuinely think · the other stuff I've been saying, on the other hand, you should take with a pinch of salt.

I make no apology for saying · things for which no one has called for me to apologise. Also 'unashamedly', for things of which no one has suggested I should be ashamed. For example, British Prime Minister David Cameron and Deputy Prime Minister Nick Clegg's statement that their 2014 legislative programme was 'unashamedly pro-work, pro-business and pro-aspirational'.

I'm not justifying it, I'm explaining it · I'm justifying it.

I'm sorry, but ... · I'm not sorry, and ....

I'm sympathetic to that proposal · I feel sorry for it, because it's doomed.

I think you'll find · that I'm right and you're wrong. But also that the depths of my loathing for you are unplumbed.

let's be honest · let's agree with me.

let's face it · let's agree you're wrong.

passionate · the standard unit of interest in a

subject. As in this IBM job ad: 'The ideal developer will be passionate about cloud computing.'

per se · ignore what I just said. As in, 'we have no plans, per se' – we have plans.

quite · means either 'very' or 'not at all', as in 'she's quite pretty'. There is a danger of accidental uncommunication here, especially when Americans are speaking to the British. Also 'some' – when Chancellor of the Exchequer Alistair Darling told US Treasury Secretary Hank Paulson in 2008 that he had 'some concerns' over Barclays buying Lehman Bros, both men thought he was being clear. Paulson thought he meant 'not very many', and Darling knew he meant 'an awful lot'.

respect · sounds like 'admire', but doesn't quite mean it. As in: 'I always had huge respect for his opinions.'

technical issues · you really don't need to worry your head about these. They're very dull.

technocrat · someone who understands the subject, but whom I wish you to ignore. Antonym: 'independent expert'.

this is the right thing to do · this is the thing we're going to do.

we do not suggest · it should be perfectly clear that we're suggesting this, but if you ask us, we'll deny it. Also 'no one disputes' – actually, we're disputing it very hard, but we're not going to admit it.

we must focus on the immediate issue · and not the thing you keep asking about.

we need a grown-up debate · I will only engage with people who agree with me.

we need to look more widely · until we find some evidence that supports my conclusions.

we rule nothing out · we're ruling lots of things out, including the thing you just said, but this isn't the moment to tell you.

we're transparent · we've inundated you with data in the hope that you'll be too busy to notice the stuff we're keeping under wraps.

we've decided to go in a different direction · from you. So please would you go in a different direction from us. Now.

what you might call · what you would call.

with respect · please die.

with the greatest respect · please die now.

without wishing to criticise · we're about to criticise someone, but it'll hurt us more than them. Probably.

you're not allowed to say this sort of thing any more · I will now disprove this statement by saying the sort of thing that I am in fact quite clearly *allowed* to say, it's just that people wish I'd stop.

A State of Undenial

The next unit of uncommunication is the Undenial, or what journalists sometimes call the 'non-denial denial'. We don't like that phrase, which was coined to describe the White House's perfectly reasonable responses to perfectly unreasonable questions following the Watergate 'incident'. However, we have to admit it's a very good description of something that sounds like a denial, but which you can point out, if cornered, actually isn't. So President Richard Nixon's press secretary Ron Ziegler would describe the *Washington Post*'s coverage as 'shabby journalism' and 'character assassination'. Its stories were based on 'hearsay, innuendo, guilt by association'.

The virtue of undenials, as *Washington Post* editor Ben Bradlee was good enough to acknowledge in his memoirs, is that most people, including many journalists, can't tell the difference. 'Some of the denials sounded technical, almost hair-splitting to us,' Bradlee wrote of his Watergate experience. 'But if it looked like a denial, smelled like a denial, and read like a denial, it was a denial, as far as the readers were concerned.'

Even when Ziegler was forced to deny his previous undenials, he found an elegant way to do it. 'This is the operative statement,' he told the Press Corps after Nixon had admitted the White House staff could have been involved in Watergate. 'The others are inoperative.'

While some of what follows applies best to those dealing with the press, it will work as well when trying to settle subordinates or put your seniors off the scent. At a pinch, they can even be used quite effectively with loved ones.*

I wouldn't hold your breath for this happening
  · because holding your breath for as long as this will take is dangerous.
I've never seen that · I've heard it, though.
I've never heard that · I've seen it, though.
that doesn't sound right · it sounds very wrong, and very true.
let me check that for you · I have no intention of checking it, or returning your call, and I'm hoping you'll somehow lose interest.
that's the most ridiculous thing I've ever heard
  · all the more so because I happen to know it's even worse than you think.

---

* To add a piece of advice from a journalist's perspective, it's best only to use one denial at a time. And not say what a press officer told one of my colleagues recently: 'The conversation never took place, and it was off the record.'

I don't recall that · memory's a sieve. Can't even remember my kids' names half the time.

I don't know for certain · which of us really knows anything *for certain*?

I'm guiding you away from that · because I don't want you to write it.

talk to your friends, see if any of them have heard that · I have misunderstood the essential quality of exclusive gossip.

I wouldn't say that if I were you. You don't want to look silly · but more importantly I don't want to look silly.

be a little bit careful where you say that · I'm hoping you might be persuaded to drop it with a vague hint that you might get into trouble for repeating it.

this is a bit old, isn't it? · are you *still* talking about last week's screw-up? Isn't it time to move on?

this is highly speculative · but, as it turns out, about right.

you're wide of the mark · but not by much.

all this has been reported before · essentially an appeal to the referee that reporters shouldn't be allowed to keep going on about the stuff you still haven't sorted out.

people are always saying this sort of thing:

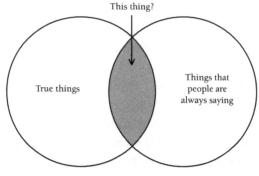

The set of all things

I don't think we have data at that level of granularity · to any request for detailed information you don't want to give up.

we don't do book reviews · on anything that's been reported in a book.

we don't comment on leaked documents · on anything based on a leaked document.

the report hasn't been published yet · on any story based on the contents of a forthcoming report.

this is overblown · if you briefed the story, but now that it's in print it doesn't look at all the way you imagined it in your head during the briefing (if someone is actually shouting at you about it, try 'totally overblown').

Finally, when issuing an undenial, be sure that it *is* an undenial:

you might think that; I couldn't possibly comment · taken from *House of Cards*, this is sometimes taken for an undenial, when in fact it's a confirmation. A sure sign that its user learned their skills from box sets. Expect them to quote *The West Wing* next.

Timing Is Everything

When are you going to get that report to me/balance the budget/fix the mower? These questions can be irritating, especially when you're stuck in the middle of a difficult level of Angry Birds, but uncomms can save you. The answer is:

as soon as possible · you think this means the next five minutes. I know it means when I get back from lunch.

soon · tomorrow. Or next month. Definitely this decade.

shortly · this covers everywhere between today and the end of the year. Or the end of next year.

before too long · though not before 'long'.

in due course · a helpful reminder to the person who's asking that things aren't as simple as just doing things. Other things have to happen first, and they shouldn't rush you.

over the coming period · a Gordon Brown favourite, this sounds very specific but is actually very vague.

in the fullness of time · an answer that gives a poetical, lyrical air to telling people that they're in for a long wait.

when the time is right · which, remember, could easily be never.

And when asked how long something will last, there's one answer that's never wrong, and never useful: **for a period of time**.

I Didn't Say This: The Unbriefing

One of the curiosities of people is that they're much more likely to believe something if they're told it in secret. It springs from a view that those of us in charge have all sorts of secret knowledge that is better than the knowledge in plain sight (and we do, of course – but nothing that we're going to share with anyone).

Take the example of journalists. Issue a statement and you'll be ignored or doubted. Hand the document to a reporter in a brown envelope, and they'll obligingly put it on the front page. Quotes so anodyne that they'd be rejected out of hand if they were attributed to a named person are repeated breathlessly when they come from a 'source'. And thanks to the honour code of reporters, they won't name their source even if the information turns out to be wrong. In fact, thanks to their vanity, they're more likely to devote their energies to explaining how, in a way, they got it right.

This brings us to the basis for the Unbriefing. Any announcement should come in two parts:

The Briefing · whether you gather people in a room, phone them up or send them an email, this is the bit where you make your formal announcement.

The Unbriefing · this is delivered afterwards to a few gossipy people, prefaced with the words: 'you didn't get this from me' or 'the bit of the story we're not telling people is ...' That will then be passed around your target audience with more efficiency, and more weight, than anything you said in the formal briefing.

An unbriefing can also be effective in circumstances when the recipient keeps it to themselves. The classic example is telling someone the size of their annual raise. That conversation should *always* open with the words: 'I shouldn't tell you, but not everyone in the company is getting this much.'

These Aren't the Unanswers You're Looking For

No good ever came of answering questions. It's not as if it even makes the people asking them happy. They just ask more questions, some of them harder than the original ones. So it's best for everyone if you just don't do it.

The most effective way of unanswering questions is not being asked them. Don't give press conferences. Don't tell journalists where you're going to be. Don't let them into the building. Cite 'security'. This is technically true, as your position will be more secure if they aren't around.

If you wish to offer a view on a subject, issue a press release, or agree with a broadcaster that you'll do a clip where you say your piece and then they leave you alone. They'll generally be so keen to keep a steady supply of such clips coming that they'll agree. If you're giving a speech and someone from the press asks a question, answer that you're keen to take questions from the audience, rather than the media. This makes you look Authentic and In Touch. On the off-chance that a member of the public has a tricky point, begin by saying that you'll take questions in groups of three, 'to get more in'. By the time you've answered the two straightforward ones, no one will be able to remember exactly what the hard question was, so pick an easy question in the same area, and answer that one. This is the true art of Uncommunication – looking open while being evasive.

If a real crisis, such as the arrest of one of your most trusted lieutenants or a natural disaster, forces you to hold a press conference, try to hold it off-camera, or somewhere where it'll be hard to send live pictures from. Rolling news editors, who'll stay with live shots of an empty podium for minutes at a time because a press conference *might* happen, are very reluctant to run recorded footage of an actual press conference that *has* happened. Keep each reporter to one question, and don't allow follow-ups. Journalists just use these to show off by pointing out that you haven't answered their question. You shouldn't give them any help with that.

You should also recruit the right kind of press officers. Look out for keen, helpful people and get rid of them. The ideal press officer will only answer the phone if one of their children has been kidnapped and they're waiting for a ransom demand. Instead, encourage them to spend time dreaming up puns to put at the top of press releases in the hope that journalists will use them.*

---

* I can confirm that these are a regular feature of press releases. Such puns are always carefully signposted inside quote marks, and possibly also in bold italic, in case anyone should fail to spot the joke.

If you rise to real prominence, you may no longer be able to get away with simply avoiding the press altogether. In that case, what you need is a spokesman. This is a person whose job is to give unanswers day after day. Ideally, they should do it in a way that is mildly entertaining but not remotely newsworthy.

Last year, one apparently humorous book listed five ways for government spokesmen to avoid questions.* It was, inevitably, incomplete.** Here is the complete Unanswers list:

I'm going to refer you elsewhere · because if you're looking for answers, you're in the wrong place.

can I get back to you? · although this might look like a promise to respond later, it's actually an existential question. To which the answer will turn out to be 'no'.

I'm not going to get into hypotheticals · one never, ever, ever has to answer questions that begin 'if'. Except like this: 'If horses had wings,

---

* Intriguingly (for me) this seems to be a reference to my own *Romps, Tots and Boffins*. Which is still in bookshops.

** This is quite true. Just after my book went to press, enterprising journalists at Yahoo News published 'The Top 9,486 Ways Jay Carney Won't Answer Your Questions', an analysis of White House press briefings, which identified thirteen types of unanswer, all of them variations on those listed here. Is it possible that President Obama's spokesman has been trained in the art of uncommunication?

they wouldn't have to shoot so many of them after the Grand National. Let's stick to reality.'

I'm not going to get into processology · it's a good word, 'processology'. It simultaneously conveys the ideas that the situation you're in is the result of a well-oiled machine functioning at its best, and that anything learned from the study of this machine will be very boring. It's unlikely that either of these things is true.

I'm not going to discuss an individual case · you can't ask me to make public comment on private individuals. And, at its heart, isn't every news story a story about private individuals?

not that I know of · if I don't know about something, I can't comment on it. Ideally, spokesmen would be sealed in sensory deprivation chambers between briefings.

I haven't discussed it with them · if the sensory deprivation tank idea isn't feasible, one should on no account hold any conversations with the person for whom one is spokesing.

I haven't seen it · in which 'it' is whichever news event you're asking me to comment on. And so I'm not going to comment on it. Go on, ask me again.

I'm not going to give a running commentary · even if I knew what was going on, letting people know would be a bad, bad idea.

HIDDEN MEANINGS

As dangerous as the unpleasant message in plain sight is the unintended second message. For reasons that probably seemed sensible at the time, the British Conservative Party chose to fight the 2005 election with the slogan: 'Are You Thinking What We're Thinking?' It was intended as a clever play on a popular phrase, suggesting that voters might find they actually agreed with the Tories more than they thought. The only flaw was the phrase's underlying meaning: 'I'm not saying what I really think.' Thus the entire election campaign became an invitation to voters to guess what it was the Tories wanted to say but weren't. The slogan appeared on the bottom of posters reading: 'It's not racist to impose limits on immigration.' Although we weren't present at the planning meetings, it seems unlikely that the message the party was aiming for was: 'we're racist, but embarrassed about it.'

I don't accept your characterisation of the situation · and I'm so offended by it that I'm not going to say another word. No, not even one.

I think I answered that yesterday · or, more precisely, if I didn't answer it yesterday, you shouldn't expect me to answer it now.

After keeping this up for ten minutes, close the conversation with the implication that, if only they'd been listening a little harder, they'd have heard something:

I think you've got what you need for your piece.

The Pivot

The worst reason in the world to talk about something is 'because they asked me about it'. People ask people about things all the time. That doesn't mean you have to blurt out answers. Instead, you need to 'pivot' from the question you've been asked to the answer you want to give. Ideally, this should be close enough to the question that people think you've dealt with it.

the really important point is · that we stop talking about the thing you're asking about.

I put these things in my own way · there's no way in Hell I'm going to agree with your proposition.

the thing I came here to talk about is · the thing that we agreed earlier, and not the thing you've just sprung on me. Back off.

I think there's a bigger issue here · like, 'what is love?' or 'is there any meaning to our existence?'

what people say to me is · uncannily, exactly what I already thought.

MAKING IT COUNT

We were distressed during the 2012 London Mayoral Election to see Boris Johnson, the incumbent, unveil a 'nine-point plan to take London forward'. Nine points is unacceptable. It looks like you couldn't be bothered to think of a tenth.

To remind you, then, these are the acceptable number of points in any rhetorical situation:

Political programmes: three, five or ten. Or one point, said three times, as in: 'Ask me my three main priorities for government and I will tell you: education, education and education.'*

Business books: three steps, or seven secrets. As in: *3 Steps To Yes: the Gentle Art Of Getting Your Way*, *5 Rules for Successful Stock Investing* and *7 Secrets of Successful Crossdressers*.**

Sermons: three points, each beginning with the same letter ('The Pre-existence of Jesus, the Pre-eminence of Jesus, the Pre-dictions of Jesus').

---

* The fact that this quote from Tony Blair in 1996 is unattributed suggests the book's authors expect a familiarity with British politics in their audience.

** These do all seem to be real books.

An advanced solution is to simply start off giving a long-winded reply to the question you would like to be answering, until you get interrupted. At this point, look grumpy, and say: **'If you'll just wait, I'm coming to your question.'** Then carry on. This puts the person who interrupted you into the wrong, and makes you appear high-minded even as you uncommunicate.

Unbusiness Meetings

Uncommunication isn't just about empty words. It's about empty gestures, too. And there's no more effective example of dynamic inaction than calling a meeting.

Our illustrious former student Herbert Hoover, powerless in the face of the Wall Street Crash and the Great Depression, showed what can be achieved by gathering great men in a room. J. K. Galbraith described how industrialists were summoned to the White House in 1929 to discuss the economy and afterwards declare their confidence in it. These meetings, Galbraith wrote, were called not because there was business to be done, but because it was necessary to create the impression business was being done. 'Such meetings are more than a substitute for action. They are widely regarded as action.'*

What was true then is true now. At the highest level, rolling news means that people can be filmed walking into the meeting, and then filmed walking out an hour later. Even on a small scale, any office can be energised by the sight of important people walking into a conference room with grim faces.

Novices sometimes worry about what will be done once the meeting is convened. There is no cause for anxiety. While the answer has changed with the march of technology – crosswords have been replaced with mobile email – few in the room will have arrived expecting to reach anything as concrete as a decision. And anyone who has risen to a senior level in a large corporation still believing that meetings exist to drive action is quite immune to evidence.

The meeting should always begin with a power-play, in which the invitees establish whose time is most valuable by seeing which of them can arrive the latest without the discussion starting in their absence. Real power is forcing eight people to make

---

* This quote is from Galbraith's *The Great Crash*. In it, Galbraith dubbed such events the 'no-business meeting'. This may be pure coincidence, and I can't find other evidence that he was aware of the skills of Uncommunication, but it does come interestingly close to what we now know to be the correct title.

ESSENTIAL UNCOMMUNICATION

small talk in a room for fifteen minutes while you sit at your computer finishing your Nespresso order.

If you think you can get away with setting up a regular meeting, you should refer to it as a 'task force'. But advanced uncommunicators may wish to consider giving every meeting a special name, perhaps based on its location. You can follow the example of those in government, and impress people simply by the location of the discussion. Obviously, there's the entry-level 'summoned to the White House', but what beats 'the President is being briefed in the Situation Room'?

The British government offers two examples of good meeting names, which were effective for different reasons. In Cold War days, when the country periodically stood on the edge of being accidentally incinerated, the important thing was that the meeting to discuss how to shut down the newspapers and what to do with all the corpses should sound dull. It was called the 'Civil Contingencies Committee'. In the new century, with the threat of mass extinction diminished, the government saw the opportunity to liven things up a bit, and the acronym COBR – for 'Cabinet Office Briefing Room' – was devised. It's crucial to the effect that this is pronounced 'cobra', as in 'deadly and coiled to strike', and not 'cobber', as in 'Australian expression of affection'. Cobra meetings, which in their early days were rare and dealt with terrorist attacks, have become more frequent, with a wider range of subjects, including tree infections. And who can blame a minister for that? Why simply have a cup of tea and a chat when you can 'convene Cobra'?

Is It a Lie If No One Believes You?

You want the top job, whether it's captaining your team or leading your country, but circumstances prevent you from saying so. Does a denial count as a lie if absolutely no one believes you? Points to consider:

- The benchmark for announcing you have no ambition is a Sherman Pledge. The original one was made by General William Sherman in 1871: 'I hereby state, and mean all that I say, that I never have been and never will be a candidate for President; that if nominated by either party, I should peremptorily decline; and even if unanimously elected I should decline to serve.' It's been popularised as: 'If drafted, I will not run; if nominated, I will not accept; if elected, I will not serve.'*

---

* I prefer the version offered by Democratic Congressman Mo Udall, who ran for the US presidency in 1976 and was asked in 1984 whether he planned to try again: 'If nominated, I shall run to Mexico. If elected, I shall fight extradition.'

- What if one wishes to leave the door open? If you want to be superficially loyal to the person whose job you're after, while still doing your best to undermine them, go for a Statement of Fact – 'There is no vacancy, we have a leader' – uttered briskly while walking past cameras. Everyone can hear the unspoken next line: '... and he's a Muppet.'

- If you want to keep the talk simmering, try a Refusal To Engage, as practised by London Mayor and perpetual Conservative Party leadership flirt Boris Johnson. Here he is, in one of many, many examples, speaking to the BBC in 2013: 'It is completely nonsensical for me to indulge this hysterical conversation. I don't want to talk about this subject.'

- A better way of leaving the door open was offered by Johnson's predecessor as wild-blond-haired Tory hopeful, Michael Heseltine. Everyone knew Heseltine wanted to replace Margaret Thatcher. Quite why he felt the need to deny it is now lost in history. The way he did it lives on: he could 'foresee no circumstances' in which he'd challenge her, he said in September 1990. Within two months, he was doing exactly that.

Questions for group discussion*

1. *The accusations that you have had a long-running affair are:*
   a) *complete balderdash*
   b) *an inverted pyramid of piffle*
   c) *all completely untrue*
   d) *ludicrous conjecture*
   e) *all of the above. And what's more, you're amazed people can write this drivel.*

2. *Five men have been caught breaking into your opponent's headquarters, with bugging equipment. Is this:*
   a) *a third-rate burglary*
   b) *something that certain elements may try to stretch beyond what it is*
   c) *something that has no place whatever in our electoral process*
   d) *a particular incident in which you have no involvement whatever?*

---

*   Interestingly, many of the 'discussion questions' in the book seem to be taken from real events and actual comments. The authors have chosen to protect the guilty, and I have respected that.

2. UNBENDING MINDS

We now turn to the art of persuasion: how to make people agree that your proposed course is 'the right thing to do'. And when we say 'right', we don't just mean 'correct'. Of course it's the case that most of you, most of the time, are making the best of a limited set of choices, none of which you may like very much. But no one wants to march under the banner of 'the least-worst option'. You should aim to invest your plan with a moral quality, so that following it is a matter of duty, a step upon the path of righteousness. This is the point of the 'mission statement', an innovation of ours so successful that it has been adopted across the business world. It may be that when you see a phrase like 'We aspire to be the world's leading maker of boiler thermostats, delivering 100 per cent customer delight', your urge is to snort with laughter. But mottoes like this elevate the humdrum into a spiritual battle.

The next logical step is to argue that your rivals are evil. Ridiculous as it may seem to an enlightened mind, this can be startlingly effective. Persuading your audience that the alternative isn't merely inferior, but actually wicked, can have devastating effects.

In this chapter, you will learn about:
➠ The Overton Window
➠ Unchoices
➠ Useful Idiots and Transitional Demands
➠ Releasing Data, and How to Avoid It
➠ Fighting Science with Doubt and Unbalance

You Can't Say That

A simple but important concept to grasp when trying to argue a case is the Overton Window.* In any debate, from diplomacy right down to the choice of restaurant for dinner, there are some proposals that are acceptable, and some that aren't. The Overton Window is the set of acceptable ideas. At the moment, for example, requiring welfare recipients to do voluntary work is inside it, but press-ganging them into the navy isn't.

The window has two important features. First, it can be in different places in different countries.

---

* The Overton Window, named after the late Joseph Overton, an American political theorist, is widely described elsewhere.

So in western Europe, it would be politically very difficult to suggest the abolition of state-funded healthcare, whereas in the US it's tough to propose its introduction.

Second, it can move. It's less than two decades since no British political party could be taken seriously if it didn't keep open the possibility of joining the euro. Today anyone advocating it would be laughed out of town.

The implications for uncommunication are twofold:

1. Work within the window. Try to shift it in your direction, by proposing ideas just inside it.

2. Move your opponents outside it. Can they be characterised as a little bit obsessed? Probably. Suggest that they're 'eccentric'. Smile while you do it. If they're on the right, do some of their ideas have a whiff of xenophobia about them? Sexism? Homophobia? Perhaps you should gently point that out. You don't need to be too shrill yourself – there's always someone ready to do that for you. If you can successfully get an opponent labelled as a 'bigot', they'll never be invited on TV again.

   If they're on the left, they'll be very sensitive

to such charges, and you may be able to use this to confuse them. Can you suggest that you yourself represent an oppressed and sympathetic minority? Or simply try to associate them with ideas whose time has passed: state planning, industrial nationalisation, more or less any left-wing politician of the 1970s or 80s. Insist that before they speak, they denounce every strike ever called, as well as the crimes of Mao, Stalin and Jimmy Hoffa.

You Don't Want to Do That

The Overton Window offers a theoretical basis for changing the terms of debate slowly, but how do we kill an idea quickly?

There's no idea so good that it can't be made to look bad with an unchoice. You just find something clearly more important or attractive, and wonder aloud whether it isn't a better thing to do. If the person proposing the original idea suggests you could do both, smile patronisingly and say 'well sure, in an ideal world, we'd do everything, wouldn't we?'

To start with, every proposal should be costed not in pounds, but in the other things you could buy instead. In government, that works according to the following price lists:

Salaries:
Nurses – £26,000
Policemen – £39,000
Teachers – £32,500

Building costs:
School – £14 million
Hospital – £500 million
Royal Navy destroyer – £1 billion

There is no limit to the number of nurses that the public think there should be. More of them is always a good thing, no matter what.* When presented with a costing, simply say: '£10 million? That's nearly 400 nurses!'

This works perfectly well in reverse, too. If you're told your proposal is too expensive, simply reply: 'Well we could afford it if we cancelled ...' and then pick the appropriate piece of unpleasantness:

Trident submarine programme – £30 billion
US Stealth Bomber programme – $81 billion

---

* There is plenty of evidence of this kind of calculation. In 2013, the *Daily Express* described one sum as enough to pay the salaries of '1.5 million nurses'.

CASE STUDY: THE UK AV REFERENDUM, 2011

The government held a referendum on changing the voting system to the Alternative Vote. The successful No campaign talked about the complication of the proposed Alternative Vote system, and its unpopularity even among those who supported reform. But the focus of their posters was the cost.

'He needs bulletproof vests NOT an alternative voting system,' one poster read, alongside a picture of a nervous-looking soldier. 'Say NO to spending £250 million on AV. Our country can't afford it.'

The British government spends around £720 billion annually. So that figure represented 0.03 per cent of one year's government spending. If that had bought a significantly better system of government, it would surely have been a good use of money.

But the genius of these posters was that they were absolutely true, totally unarguable, and completely beside the point. Of course a soldier needs body armour more than he needs a different voting system. And yet wouldn't it be possible for him to have *both*? In Britain's AV referendum, the Yes campaign never managed to find a way of saying that, which is why the No campaign, which focused on the essentially negligible costs of the proposed system, won convincingly.

It's important to note at this point that you probably won't be comparing fairly: nurses like to get
paid every year, whereas many spending projects
arc one-offs: once you've built a new railway line,
you don't need to build it again. Note it, and then
make the comparison anyway. This isn't a textbook
about fighting fair.

It's unlikely, of course, that the person proposing to build an airport down the road from you is
actually planning to lay off nurses to pay for it. Governments have quite a lot of money, and are capable
of spending it on several things at once. But that
doesn't stop this being a successful tactic.

Groucho or Karl?

We now turn to Marxism. This isn't a point about
political systems – they all have their uses, and
they're generally beneath us. But nobody argues
like a Marxist. Here are two particularly useful ideas
we've borrowed from the revolution:

Useful Idiots

No public campaign is complete without a letter
signed by fifty chief executives. And if you can't get
fifty chief executives to sign your letter, you ought

to give up. Look at it this way: only five of them need to be big names; the rest will be described as 'and forty-five others' anyway, so they're really just padding. They don't even need to actually support your campaign. After a life spent selling cheap shirts or manufacturing carburettors, many of them will be flattered to be asked to contribute to the national debate. They just need to be presented with a text that they can sign. When you release it to the media, you can call the journalists to explain what it really means.

If they're still reluctant, offer to add the words 'signed in a personal capacity' after their name. This translates as: 'I am a senior executive, and I have added my name to a campaigning letter. Everyone in my company thinks I'm an idiot for doing so. I have been convinced by the campaign group that adding this phrase to my signature will in some way distance my company from the campaign. Everyone in my company thinks I'm an idiot for believing that, too.'

If your signatories are upset by the way the letter is reported, their first response will be to blame the press for misunderstanding the letter, rather than themselves for being gulled. Even if they should possess enough insight to realise they were used, they're unlikely to want to admit it.

Transitional Demands

The ideal text for such a letter will contain a request that is superficially reasonable, but actually unattainable. After building broad but shallow support for your initial position (tourists to be kept off metropolitan transport networks during peak hours, parenting classes for people on welfare) you wait for it to be rejected, and then announce that this just goes to show what's really needed is your actual goal (tourists shot at the border, enforced sterilisation of the poor). Having signed up to your initial position, you aim to bring a portion of your supporters with you the rest of the way, if only out of politeness.

Attack Uncommunications

Whether you wish to destroy a person or their idea, there comes a moment when it's necessary to go on the offensive. Here we provide the ammunition for your assault.

a real danger · there is no danger of this happening at all.

bigot · someone who holds views as strong as ours, but in the opposite direction.

check your privilege · a phrase used in left-wing debates on the internet to signal that this has now turned into a Top Trumps-style competition in which the person who's suffered the most discrimination will win.

courageous · stupid.

creeping · someone is doing something with which we disagree, but slowly. If they're doing it quickly, it's 'rushed'.

damning criticism · what you expect any inquiry into these incidents to produce. When it doesn't, that will be because it was a 'whitewash'.

diktat · statement with which I disagree.

dossier · any collection of allegations that we have written down.

far enough · where today's otherwise welcome announcement by our opponents doesn't, sadly, go.

for too long · the period of time for which we have had to put up with whatever it is we're attacking.

gimmick · popular idea we wish we'd thought of.

ideological · someone with fixed ideas whom we dislike. If we *do* like them, try 'committed'.

idly by · the manner in which people with whom you disagree are standing, and the stance you typically cannot manage.

ilk · people standing near someone we dislike.

illegal war · foreign policy decision with which we disagreed, either at the time or in retrospect.

imposed · the means by which things of which we disapprove are implemented.

industrial · the scale on which bad things have been happening.

misguided · their intentions are good, but they're idiots.

proper process · what now needs to be 'put in place' instead of the 'frankly inadequate' one set up by our opponent.

questions to answer · what your opponent still has after today's announcement.

slap in the face for victims · what today's announcement by our opponents generally is.

time and again · when this undesirable thing has happened.

too little, too late · the quality of our opponents' proposals when they're in serious danger of being popular.

unfettered · a good way of making something that people might otherwise be in favour of, such as capitalism or globalisation, sound like a dangerous thing.

what, and when · the question is generally who knew this.

wilfully · the manner in which your opponent ignored warnings.

worrying · the nature of a report which makes

no specific criticisms. If it's a long report, try
'extremely worrying'. If it actually *is* worrying,
use 'disturbing'.

yawning · the quality of the gap between what our
opponent promised and what they've delivered.

zealot · one who strongly holds views different from
my own strongly held views.

Just Asking Questions

There are assertions that you cannot make and keep
your credibility: that President Obama was born in
Nigeria, not Hawaii; that Tony Blair ordered the
killing of a government scientist; that stock trad-
ers, or the Israelis, or the US Air Force knew about
or organised the 9/11 attacks. However, you may be
able to keep these in the public mind while distanc-
ing yourself from them. You do this by saying you're
'just asking questions'.

Why are you asking questions? Because 'people
want their minds put at rest', of course. Sadly, they
won't achieve this peace, because the questions are
never-ending. In the US, the leading just-askers
of questions are Glenn Beck and Donald Trump.
In Britain, the job is undertaken by a crack team
at the *Daily Mail* newspaper, who raise such
issues as:

Is This Ancient Egyptian Statue a Sign There Really Is a Curse of the Pharaohs?

Is This Proof the Virgin Queen Was an Imposter in Drag?

Did China or Jihadists Try to Bankrupt America?

Did MI6 Agent Kill Spy in Bag?

Is This a Squadron of UFOs Flying Over California?*

Persuasion Through Titles

In the beginning are words, and the words become projects. And those projects can succeed or fail depending on who has the best words for them. One should never embark upon a potentially unpopular course of action without having a name for it that makes it sound not just reasonable, but right. If you don't come up with one, your opponents will.

We have advised both sides in the debate about abortion in the US, resulting in the adoption, since the 1970s, first of 'pro-choice' and then 'pro-life'.

---

* Some of these *Daily Mail* headlines seem to be taken from my colleague John Rentoul's excellent book, *Questions to Which the Answer Is 'No!'*.

Most people are, of course, generally in favour of both 'life' and 'choice'.

We look on in admiration at the work done in the US to rebrand estate duty as the 'death tax'. In the UK, Margaret Thatcher made an effort to make an unpopular tax change palatable by calling it 'the Community Charge'. She was outmatched by her opponents, who came up with the snappier 'poll tax', a name that even her supporters now use. Her successors were blindsided and forced to retreat when a reclassification of some hot foods in 2012 was named by opponents as 'the pasty tax'.

But names can't just kill a project. They can also make it irresistible. In more primitive ages, people gave laws boring but meaningful titles, such as 'The Tenants' Rights, Etc. (Scotland) Act 1980' or, in the US, boring but meaningless ones, such as 'The Glass-Steagall Act'. As these titles are used whenever people refer to the bills, this seemed to us a waste of a branding opportunity. So we're pleased to have successfully introduced a range of more useful titles, which have proved especially effective in education. Who, for instance, could vote against the 'No Child Left Behind Bill'? Someone who wanted children left behind, that's who. In the UK, an improvement programme was made harder to cut by calling it 'Building Schools for the Future'.

Had we realised the effectiveness of this technique sooner, it would have avoided much unpleasant criticism:

Breaking Down Barriers Between Faith Groups
· the Crusades.

Sustainable Families Through Wider Engagement · Henry VIII's marital strategy.

Opportunities for Tomorrow in Eastern Saxony · the bombing of Dresden.

Building Diverse Communities · apartheid.

Creating Critical Mass to Drive Demand for Safe Technology · Chernobyl.

Our Survey Said

If you want to win an argument, there's nothing better than being able to show that you have the people on your side. You don't just want to assert that, of course; you want scientific proof.

A good way is to commission a poll to show that people support you. This is quite different from commissioning a poll to find out what people think.

There are a number of amateur ways to achieve this. The easiest is simply to allude airily to 'private polling' which proves your point. Don't give numbers or any details that would allow anyone to check what you say. This is popular with anyone trying to sell an unpopular product or person, which is why political parties use it so much. It can typically be seen in the second half of the sixth paragraph of a news story, thus: 'Campaign strategists say their private polling suggests the outcome is much more finely balanced.' As you have already seen, the word 'secret' has a strange effect on your audience, and they will accept unquestioningly the idea that an unpublished poll that asked exactly the same question as the public polls would come up with a different, and more reliable, answer. If your listener is slightly more perceptive than average, and queries this, simply reply: 'A lot depends on how you ask the question.' Which, as we'll see, has the merit of being true.

The next level up, in that the poll is actually conducted, is the 'write-in poll'. This is any one where you simply announce you're doing a poll and ask people to respond by post, email or phone. As the respondents are self-selecting, the results are worthless, except to prove a point to an uncritical audience. They also run the risk of producing results that resemble a North Korean election in their one-sidedness. Too overwhelming, and a poll looks unconvincing. But dressed up correctly, such polls can look plausible. Business lobby groups often send out mass emails to members, collate the responses, and then announce 'Senior executives oppose taxing company cars by four-to-one!' Few will bother to dig into the data to establish how the few hundred executives who took part in the poll came to do so. Marketing companies, meanwhile, will email thirty of their friends, ask them about shampoo, and then concoct a press release.

But if you want your poll to have real heft, consider commissioning a proper survey of a randomly selected group.

It might seem that this is only a good idea if your idea does have public support, but as we shall see, there are polls and polls.

One option is a simple 'what would you think IF ...' question. There's a chance that if you ask it enough times, you'll get the result you want. It doesn't mean much, because people are quite bad at judging their future behaviour. In July 2011, looking at Republican candidates for the presidential race, Harris Interactive polled 2,183 adults and announced that 'President Obama Would Lose if Mitt Romney or Rudy Giuliani Was the Nominee'. Or not, as it turns out. But how could the people Harris interviewed know? Only 29 per cent of them described themselves as 'very familiar' with Romney. By the time the election came round fifteen months later, people knew a lot more about him, and they'd changed their minds.

There's a different problem with 'state-of-the-race' polling. It generally produces consistent results, but the difficulty is interpreting them. In Britain, people are asked almost daily how they would vote if there were a general election tomorrow. The trouble is that 1,825 days out of every 1,826, there isn't a general election tomorrow. And the people answering the question know that. The question they answer instead is: 'How do you feel about the government in general, and are there any politicians you'd especially like to kick?' Even those who engage with the question face the problem that, as with Americans and Mitt Romney, they just don't know how they're going to feel at the end of an election campaign that's months or years away.

So what do you do if straightforward polls show that people don't much like your idea? Time to ask some leading questions. In February 2014, London's Underground rail network was shut down for two days by a strike. The strikers pointed to a poll that showed the public supported them and opposed management's plans to change staff roles and cut jobs. Management pointed to their own survey that showed the public supported their plan. How could that be?

Here's the question asked in the management poll:

Today, due to Oyster and other innovations, just 3 per cent of Tube journeys involve a visit to a ticket office. So in future, Transport for London proposes that staff are moved from inside ticket offices to ticket halls and platforms where they can provide the best face-to-face service to customers. As a result, there will be more staff visible and available to help customers buy the right ticket, plan their journeys and keep them safe and secure. Transport for London is committed to delivering this change with no compulsory redundancies.

Got all that? As it turns out, an astonishing 82 per cent thought it was a good idea to 'provide the best face-to-face service', 'help customers buy the right ticket' and 'keep them safe and secure'. Possibly more interestingly, 12 per cent thought those things sounded like a bad idea.

But what about the union poll? It asked a series of questions. First:

'To what extent would you or would you not be concerned if the tube stations on your journey no longer had manned ticket offices?'

Now, the preamble pointed out that this wasn't

the management plan, but the question is the bit people pay attention to, because that's the bit they have to answer. It turns out that 76 per cent of people would be concerned.

Next:

'Do you think that the Mayor of London should speak directly with trade unions without preconditions if that meant strike action on the tube could be prevented?'

The most surprising thing about the answer was that 10 per cent said no – one person in ten thought that *if* a simple meeting would prevent a large amount of inconvenience for millions, it *still* shouldn't happen. These probably overlapped with the 12 per cent who thought that Underground staff shouldn't keep customers safe.

Finally:

'Do you think that lawful industrial action as a last resort is justified in these circumstances?'

The question didn't specify what the 'circumstances' were, but those interviewed could probably work out that they were the closure of ticket offices and a mayor who refused to hold meetings that would stop strikes. And this question was about 'lawful industrial action as a last resort'. Which, we learn, two-thirds of people support.

CASE STUDY: THE BEST EVER LEADING QUESTION

The undisputed high point of leading questions came in a survey conducted in London in 2005, as part of the bid to host the 2012 Olympics, when it was important to demonstrate public support:

> *To what extent do you agree with Nelson Mandela's view that, because London is a diverse city, providing a home to hundreds of nationalities, it would be the best place to hold the Olympic Games?*

It turns out that, in polls, 72 per cent of Londoners agreed with the most popular man on earth.

Selling Doubt

There's no such thing as a lost cause. Several decades ago, some of our members were approached by tobacco companies disturbed by the suggestion that, far from delivering throat comfort, cigarettes might actually be killing people. What was more, the government wanted to put warnings on their packets saying as much. Were they doomed? Should they get out of the nicotine business and start selling something that saved lives, like asbestos, or fossil fuels?

Happily, we were able to relieve their concerns. Restrictions on cigarette sales have increased over the years, of course, but we've got nowhere near a ban, and the battle against them has lasted careers. Lifetimes even, in the case of some heavy users of the product.

How were we able to achieve this, in the face of overwhelming scientific evidence? Well, we developed a model so successful that we've repeated it since in the fight against other science-based attacks on industry, from the asbestos industry to global-warming obsessives.

It is somewhat unfortunate that, in the course of the development of the plan, some parts of it were written down. It is a source of even greater regret that the document then found its way into the public domain. The articulation of the strategy, however, is sound. The tobacco giants weren't just selling cigarettes any more. They were selling uncertainty:

'Doubt is our product since it is the best means of competing with the "body of fact" that exists in the mind of the general public. It is also the means of establishing a controversy.'*

---

* This is a quote from a 1969 document obtained from the tobacco company Brown & Williamson. The authorship of the original document is uncertain, but it can be found in a number of online archives kept by anti-smoking groups.

Here, threatened by science, we use the scientific method against itself. Science conducts itself on a plane removed from ordinary people. Ordinary people, in turn, don't really trust scientists. They like the magic things they make, but at any given moment, they're only one mutant cow away from burning the faculty of the Massachusetts Institute of Technology at the stake for witchcraft. You can see this whenever there's a medical scare. No amount of doctors and professors paraded on the television announcing that a vaccine is safe will reassure the anxious populace.

This is partly because of the language in which science is conducted. Like us, scientists have special meanings for words that are in ordinary use. Unlike us, they don't grasp the effect of this. When they use a word like 'theory', they mean 'testable and well-tested idea that explains the observed facts'. They don't realise that the public hears 'guess'.

So you don't *deny* that smoking causes cancer, or that carbon dioxide is contributing to global warming. Simply point out that it's 'unproven', and then say that 'conclusive proof' is needed before costly decisions are made on the basis of something that's really 'just a theory'. Scientists, who, like a lot of very clever people, are also a bit stupid, won't respond by stabbing your eyes out with a test tube. Instead, they will take up the challenge, and go off and do another five years of research. You should welcome this, as it suits your next argument: that 'more research is needed'. Note that you don't need to back this up by actually funding research. Not the research of your opponents, anyway.

The research you should support is the research of your supporters. You can always find someone with a scientific qualification who'll say what you want, so long as you're not too fussy. And you will need them when you deploy the next weapon in our arsenal: Unbalance.

Such debates are conducted through the press, and the press prides itself on balance. So when they put up a climate expert explaining what the vast majority of climate scientists think, insist they put up a physicist you provide to argue that none of this is proven. The public is used to hearing two politi-cians arguing and then concluding that the answer is somewhere in between them. When they hear two scientists debate, they come to the same conclusion. The other side may have 99 per cent of the experts on their side, but the rules of public debate give your side equal weight.

CASE STUDY: CLIMATE CHANGE

You don't even need a scientist. In February 2014, for a debate on whether increasingly extreme weather was linked to carbon dioxide emissions, the BBC settled for Nigel Lawson, a former Chancellor of the Exchequer, to put the case against. The close of the discussion showed just how effective this use of balance can be for us. The climate expert asserted that excess energy was being absorbed by the oceans; the conversation concluded thus:

Lawson: That is pure speculation.
Scientist: No, it's a measurement.
Lawson: No, it's not. It's speculation.
BBC presenter: Well, it's a combination of the two, isn't it?

Unbalance: your friend in the fight against science.

Publish and Be Damned

'Openness' is the uncommunicator's watchword. Which is to say that it's a word you should watch out for. While describing oneself as 'open' at every opportunity is a basic part of uncommunication, be careful you don't confuse that with actually being open. Listen to the wisdom of Tony Blair, who got carried away one day and introduced a Freedom of Information Act to Britain: 'There is really no description of stupidity, no matter how vivid, that is adequate. I quake at the imbecility of it.'*

People who make Freedom of Information requests fall into two categories:

1. Journalists.
2. Weirdos.

These are not mutually exclusive categories.

Neither of these groups is interested in using anything that they find out to prove that you're doing a good job in difficult circumstances. As Blair also says, releasing information to them is 'like saying to someone who is hitting you over the head with a stick, "Hey, try this instead", and handing them a mallet'.

In such circumstances, holding information back is more or less your duty, to ensure fairness. When the press starts putting your successes on the front page, you can consider telling them what you've got wrong.

But you can't simply say 'we're not telling you', not when 'openness' is your watchword. Instead your message should be 'we'd love to tell you, but ...'

---

* This quote, and the one below it, are taken from Blair's memoirs, *A Journey*, in a section where the former prime minister describes the Freedom of Information Act as one of his two great domestic mistakes (the other was banning fox-hunting).

This communication should be dragged out as much as possible. If the law gives you twenty-eight days to reply, take twenty-eight days. Journalists get bored quickly, and there's a good chance they'll forget they asked the question in the first place, and move on. Sadly, weirdos (and weirdo journalists) are not so easily shaken off.

These are your lines of defence:

Commercial confidentiality · we'd love to give you the data, but we've made promises to other people that mean it's not our secret to tell.

Someone else is already looking at it · we wouldn't want you to go to the trouble of looking at all this data, when it's already being looked at elsewhere. It's terribly dull, believe us.

Here's a little bit; are you happy now? · The release of small amounts of data enables you to say that you're 'cooperating'. If anyone asks, you roll your eyes and say, 'look, the weirdos asked for data, and we gave them data, and now they're saying they want more data. Have you noticed they're a bit weird?'

Oh, wasn't that everything you wanted? · We honestly thought it was. So sorry. Can't imagine how that happened. Now, what was it you wanted again?

WOULD THEY LIE TO YOU?

CASE STUDY: TAMIFLU

In 2009, a group of doctors trying to establish the effectiveness of the influenza drug Tamiflu realised that trials had been conducted on it whose results had never been published. They wrote to Roche, the drug's makers, requesting access to the data. Roche promised to make 'full study reports' available 'within the coming days'. They nevertheless managed not to hand the data over for more than three years, all the while saying they were committed to 'greater transparency'. Their reticence was fully justified. When the doctors did get their hands on the data, they were somewhat sniffy about whether the billions of dollars governments had put towards stockpiling Tamiflu was money well spent.*

We can't trust you with it · by this stage, the person requesting the data has generally mouthed off, giving the opportunity to suggest that perhaps they aren't really the sort of people who could be trusted with sensitive information.

---

* The 'group of doctors' referred to here is the Cochrane Collaboration. They published their report into Tamiflu in 2014, saying the evidence they obtained from Roche showed the drug 'shortens symptoms of influenza by half a day' but with 'increased risk of suffering from nausea and vomiting'. Interestingly, a reading of the correspondence between Cochrane and Roche features all of the stages listed here, as well as long delays in replying to requests.

By definition, anyone still requesting information after the previous four stages is an obsessive. And if they weren't weird at the start of stage one, you'll have driven them weird by now.

You're talking to journalists · of course they are. The kind of people who doggedly pursue data are the same kind of people who write to journalists. And if there's one group of people who really shouldn't be trusted with sensitive data, it's the press.

Remember that even if all you do is stall for a few years, that's not time wasted.

Putting It Out There

Although your general rule should be not to release data, sometimes it's a good idea. It makes you look open, and it can support your case. That doesn't mean you should publish *all* your data. But there can be a strong case for publishing the bits that prove your point.

Take, again, our friends in the pharmaceutical industry. They have to run dozens of trials in order to prove their drugs work and are safe. And they never forget that this is why they pay for the trials: to prove their drugs work and are safe. No one's interested in results that suggest they're not safe or they don't work. No one who's paying for trials, anyway. A 2010 study found that the results of only half of drug trials are published. And positive results are twice as likely to be published as negative ones.

They're helped in this by a phenomenon called 'publication bias'. Science journals are more interested in papers that show interesting new results than those that show a lack of them. It turns out that although a key principle of science is supposed to be testing and disproving theories, publishers of scientific results don't find disproofs as exciting as proofs.

It's not just science journals that behave that way. The whole world is more attracted to shiny new things than boring old things. Use that. Offer to show the person you're trying to persuade 'unpublished' or 'preliminary' results. We know these words mean 'unchecked' and 'quite possibly wrong', but your target will hear 'secret' and 'brand new'. This is especially effective with journalists, who can be given your personal interpretation of the data, without any pointy-heads offering a more sober alternative.

Questions for group discussion

1. *In an effort to cash in on the bottled water craze, you're selling treated tap water. It now seems that the treatment process adds a carcinogen to the water. Is the withdrawal of your product:*
   a) *a precautionary measure*
   b) *made despite there being no 'immediate' health risk?*

2. *The link between human activity and global warming is:*
   a) *extremely speculative and uncertain*
   b) *only so widely believed because of media bias and brainwashing*
   c) *agreed by 97 per cent of climate scientists.*

3. UNDAMAGE CONTROL

Triumph and disaster may well both be imposters, but it would be a great mistake to treat them just the same. While triumphs are things for which you should try at all costs to take the credit, disasters are things for which a certain skill is required to avoid any blame. Where blame cannot be shifted, you may have to issue an unapology, but we can ensure that those demanding it don't enjoy it.

In this chapter, you will learn about:
➡ Unexpectations
➡ The Ten Lines of Defence
➡ The Unapology
➡ How to Demand an Apology

Great Unexpectations

The first phase in dealing with bad news is preparing the ground. The technique is so simple that children quickly learn it: make your audience think things are going to be worse than they are. The brain anchors itself on to the first piece of information it receives, and then judges new information relative to that. So if you're told that something should usually cost £1,000, but today is only £950, there's an inclination to think 'oh, cheap!'

Managing unexpectations shouldn't be left to chance. Once you have a good idea of how badly things are going to turn out, generate a significantly worse estimate and unbrief it through your most effective channels.

While You're There ...

Another seemingly trivial uncommunication skill is the timing of the release of news you control. If you have low-level bad news to put out, make sure it goes at a time when your audience is already busy. If one presents itself, use a big news day, such as an election or a royal wedding. If no such opportunity presents itself, create a busy day by releasing lots of information at once, ideally close to deadlines. But, and we cannot emphasise this enough, do not announce in an email your intention to bury news.*

---

* This seems to be a reference to the British ministerial aide who sent the following message to colleagues on the afternoon of 11 September 2001: 'It's now a very good day to get out anything we want to bury.'

ATTENTION TO DETAIL

Any attack on you is only as strong as its weakest point. If you can find a single factual error in the case against you, you should shout about it from the roof-tops. Has a government scientist who specialises in secret work been described as an intelligence source? That's enough of a distinction to discredit a report based on their words.

The Ten Lines of Defence

Everyone makes mistakes. Only the weak need be destroyed by them. Keep your head, and follow our tried-and-tested plan:

The first line of defence · nothing happened.

The second line of defence · everyone calm down. You need to define your event using the most boring words possible. Ideally, you want several words, all of them containing several syllables, and adding up to something in the passive voice. You didn't 'crash', you were 'in collision'. It wasn't the start of an 'eight-car pile-up', it was a 'multiple vehicle incident'. With 'fatalities'.

The third line of defence · you take full responsibility. This is a precise meaning of responsibility that specifically excludes any blame. Instead your implication is that you're taking responsibility for clearing up some other idiot's mess. But that you don't want thanks – you're just doing your job.

The fourth line of defence · no one could have foreseen this. If there are people who did, point out that it's very difficult to know when you should believe people who're always predicting disaster (as in: 'yeah, well he's predicted eight of the last two recessions'). Remember: it was no use someone telling you that the bridge was bound to collapse one day. You needed to be told which day it would collapse.

The fifth line of defence · it's no one's fault. A 'blame game' isn't going to help anyone. It's not going to help you, anyway. Announce an internal inquiry that will report in private, at some distant, unspecified time. Then refuse to answer any more questions until that inquiry has finished its work.

The sixth line of defence · it's someone else's fault. If we are going to have a blame game, we have to win it. Good people to blame are your predecessor (unless they're now your boss) or your political opponent. You should never blame the victim, and you should point out that you're not blaming the victim at every opportunity. As in:

'I know there's a lot of muttering that what happened to this moron is in some way this moron's fault. Well that stops right here. I take full responsibility for what this moron managed to do to himself.'

The seventh line of defence · it was your assistant's fault. You've been let down by people in whom you had put your faith. Frankly, they betrayed your trust, and you're shocked to find out what they did. Steer round questions about why they might have concluded you would approve of their actions. The big point is that you're appalled.

The eighth line of defence · it was your fault, but not really. You weren't yourself. This was never your intention. You were poorly advised. If you're on prescription painkillers whose side effects include blackouts, consider whether this may be the time to mention it.

The ninth line of defence · look, a puppy! Look for a trivial but endearing detail to subvert your critics. Richard Nixon proved a master of this when faced with a political funding scandal in 1952. In a TV address, he moved the subject from the money to a dog that had been sent to his daughters by a supporter. 'Our little girl – Tricia, the six-year-old – named it Checkers,' he told a weeping nation. 'And you know, the kids, like all kids, love the dog and I just want to say this right now, that regardless of what they say about it, we are going to keep it.'*

The last line of defence · it was your fault, but you have nothing to apologise for. At this stage, a bold bid to get back to the first line is worth a shot. Once again, Nixon is our model, with his argument that 'when the president does it, that means that it is not illegal'.

Defensive Uncommunication

As you circle the wagons, language can help to deflect even the best-aimed attack. These are the phrases you'll need to draw upon.

a different era · when, you have to understand, the things we're talking about took place. Who would have guessed that groping strangers would turn out to have been wrong thirty years later?

a mixed picture · a total disaster.

a number of root causes are being investigated · we have absolutely no idea what happened.

---

* Nixon was lying about the money, but the broadcast was devastatingly effective. Well-wishers sent cash and enough dog food to keep Checkers going for a year.

an incident of concerted indiscipline · a riot.*

artificial deadline · the sort that won't help this situation.

distraction from the important issue · the nature of the thing that people keep asking about. It may also be a 'storm in a teacup'.

hindsight is a wonderful thing · while it's true that we have made a terrible mistake, we want to label anyone who points this out as a little bit stupid and unbearably smug.

innocent mistake · one of which we are entirely guilty, though we hope to pretend otherwise.

lessons must be learned · yes, this is a disaster, but the important thing is to recognise it's not my fault.

only one · the number of results that really count. Typically deployed after a result that might otherwise have counted has gone against us.

out of context · how we were quoted.

personal reasons · the standard explanation for leaving a job. Generally the reason being that the person in charge wanted me, personally, gone.

pre-empt the process of the investigation · what I'm not going to do, by commenting on the thing on which you want me to comment. The point of

---

* This is indeed how a 2014 breakdown of order at one of Britain's largest prisons was described by the company in charge.

announcing an investigation is to make an issue go away until everyone has forgotten about it, so offering fresh comment would rather defeat the point.

private · a matter that I don't wish to discuss because it's none of your business. A matter that someone else doesn't wish to discuss is 'secret'.

smear · a reminder of a truth about me that I don't like.

tawdry · my opponent's tactics may be effective, but I think you should look down on them anyway.

that's deeply patronising · I'm not going to dispute your conclusion, but I think you should feel bad for reaching it.

the important thing is · not the thing you just asked me about.

this is a very divisive position · I disagree with this decision, and wish other people would, too.

unduly affected · what people won't be by whatever's just gone wrong. They will be 'duly affected', of course.

valuable lessons · the sort that I've learned, generally about myself, during the 'time of reflection' I've had after the episode from which I'd like everyone to now move on.

we regret · we're sorry that people are upset about the thing that we did that we're not sorry we did.

A game of two halves

Football managers are generally particularly skilled at explaining away failure, partly because they get a lot of public practice.*

a few key decisions have cost us today · it's the referee's fault we lost.

compete with their resources · what we can't do, when we wish to justify our failure to beat a rich club.

it was a turning point in the game · we had one chance and missed it, and were then thrashed.

didn't see it at the time · the reason we can't comment on our centre back breaking the leg of the opposition striker in the penalty area.

the conditions made it difficult for both sides · it was raining slightly.

they made it difficult for us · they were better than us.

they play in a certain way which is hard to deal with at times · they should all be banned for life.

the positives · what we'll take from this defeat. Though the negatives might be more useful.

---

* If football managers and players are in fact trained in uncomms, it would certainly explain why their interviews are all so dull.

Regrets? Too Few to Mention

From time to time, all of us will be called upon to say sorry for something we've done or said. This is bad enough if we are sorry. But one of the indignities of modern life is the demands for retraction of remarks that we think are true, and with which most people privately agree, but that are for some reason deemed unacceptable.

In such circumstances, the quickest way to escape with honour satisfied may be an unapology. When composing yours, the model should be a railway announcement that a train has been cancelled, with the accompanying regret 'for any inconvenience caused'. The implication should hang in the air that, though you are indeed apologising, you're doing so out of politeness, because what happened was really nobody's fault.

The key to a good unapology is that those who wanted you to give it should be simultaneously unsatisfied and unable to say what it lacks. Too *fulsome* and you'll have let them win; too *grudging* and they'll be able to demand more.

So if the nation's geography teachers are calling for your dismissal after you accused them of 'perverting young minds with their maps', you need something like this:

'I'm sorry if ...' · open by making it clear your apology is conditional. And conditional on something that probably isn't true. In which case, you're not sorry at all.

'... offence was caused ...' · keep it passive. If, and we're not saying there was, but if there was offence, it was just something that happened, not the result of deliberate actions.

'... by my remarks' · key moment here to define what it is that you're not exactly apologising for. And it's never too late to downgrade. Don't call it a 'speech' if you can get away with 'comments'. And any book under 300 pages can probably be passed off as a 'pamphlet'.

'I have huge respect for teachers' · now move on, with an expression of general admiration for the people you may or may not have offended. If you simply cannot abide them, try to find a superset to which they belong of which you are fond. It needs to be a little narrower than: 'I've always liked humans.'

'There are thousands of them working hard, up and down the country' · good moment for a Statement of Fact.

'I wouldn't want to give them offence' · nice swerve here. Grammatically, this is a reference to the thousands of teachers who work hard.

But the map-peddling geography sickos will probably think it refers to them.

'I hope this will be an end to the matter' · and that's all they're getting from you. The circus can move on. And surprisingly often, it will.

How to Demand an Apology

The situation is much happier if the boot is on the other foot. If an opponent has been foolish enough to express a view about something, crucify them for it. You'll need:

- **Timing:** Demands for apologies are generally poor news stories, so you need to do it at a quiet time. Saturdays are good: partly because this is when newspapers tend to run long interviews in which someone may have said something off-guard, but also because there isn't much news around, and Sunday-paper reporters may be grateful for a decent row to fill a bit of space the next day. Likewise Sundays, when the few people dragging stuff together for Monday's paper are desperate for anything to get them home. If your apology-demand is really weak, consider whether it'll keep until Christmas.

- **The least-charitable interpretation possible:** Is there a way in which your opponent's comment that the hospital should have noticed one of their nurses was killing patients could be interpreted as AN ATTACK ON ALL HEALTH PROFESSIONALS? No? Look again. Can you see it yet?

- **Outrage:** Your outrage won't do. You ideally need a representative of the 'victims'. Fortunately most people who might take such a role have learned that those who shout loudest get rewarded.

- **An open letter:** You should now write, in tones of mixed sorrow and anger, to your opponent or, better yet, their boss. Obviously an actual letter would be too slow – an emailed document will be fine. But do remember to send it to the recipient *before* you release it to the press. The most damning put-down to such epistles is 'I don't think we've actually received it yet'.

With a couple of press releases and a fair wind, this is enough to produce a 'row' or a 'calls for apology' story. And coverage was all you wanted, right?

The Black Death – An Apology

While you should avoid apologising for things you have done, there's a lot to be said for contrition about things that aren't your fault. It costs nothing, tickles some tummies, and may enable you to take a sideswipe at your predecessor while appearing noble. There are also so many things to choose from. To offer a few national examples:

Australia · Fosters lager

Denmark · The final four plot twists of each series of *The Killing*

France · The Norman invasion of England in 1066

Greece · The sacking of Troy

Iraq · The destruction of Jerusalem by the Babylonians

Israel · Ethnic cleansing of Canaanites, Hittites, Girgashites, Amorites, Perizzites, Hivites, and Jebusites

Italy · The rape of the Sabine women

Japan · Pearl Harbour, 1941

Sweden · The layout of Ikea stores

UK · Burning the White House in 1814. It was beneath us, really.*

USA · *Pearl Harbor*, 2001

---

* David Cameron did actually apologise for this, during a 2012 visit to Washington.

Questions for group discussion

Consider your response to the following situations:

1. *You are the governor of a US state. After a slight by a town mayor, your staff diverted large amounts of traffic through that mayor's town. How inconceivable is it that you knew nothing about it, and how many underlings will you have to throw overboard to avoid blame?*

2. *You are a Member of Parliament whose expense claims are under scrutiny. Is this because:*
    a) *The public are jealous of your very, very large house, which is sometimes compared to Balmoral*
    b) *The whole system is rotten, and it needs to change. You have been a part of that system, and you apologise for that*
    c) *People are effectively saying you should only be allowed to buy things from a 99p store?*

4. CREATING AN UNIMPRESSION

Good name in man or woman is the immediate jewel of their soul. It's also a vital aid for future uncommunication: people are more likely to believe us when they already think we're trustworthy. And uncomms can in turn help to deliver such a reputation.

It's an interesting feature of the human that we make our judgements very quickly, and then are reluctant to abandon them. Psychologists have shown that we look for evidence to confirm our judgements and struggle to process evidence that contradicts them. So if you can just give people the idea you're trustworthy or clever or polite, you'll be able to spend years being unreliable, stupid and rude without them reversing these assessments.

In this chapter, you will learn about:
➡ Taking the Credit
➡ Avoiding the Blame
➡ Unpledges
➡ Winning at Twitter

Credit Where It's Undue

True success is the result of talent, good luck and hard work. Two of those you can't count on, and the other one is a lot of effort. Much better to take credit for a success that has already happened, ideally one close to where you were standing.

This is the trick played by your bosses when, in the face of their best efforts to absent-mindedly sabotage your project, it succeeds. Before you know it, they're circulating memos about their team's triumph. It happens at every level. During the boom years of financial services, senior bank executives were happy to take credit – and money – for profits made in parts of their organisations that it would later emerge they didn't understand at all.

The masters are politicians. While Harold Wilson was joking when he observed that England's football team 'only ever win the World Cup under a Labour government', Tony Blair and Gordon Brown were quite serious when they argued that the low inflation and interest rates enjoyed in the UK under their governments were the result of their decision to grant the Bank of England independence.* They

---

* Alan Greenspan suggested in his memoirs that the collapse of communism, leading to the arrival of a billion low-paid workers on the global jobs market, along with their increasing savings, may have been more of a factor.

never explained how this 1997 decision also led to similarly low rates in the USA and Europe, and they were never seriously challenged on it.

The essential ingredients to doing this successfully are:

getting in early · you need to make your move just before it's clear to everyone that something is definitely going to be a triumph.

getting it in writing · your name has to be on the work somewhere. If that means taking off the name of someone more deserving, reassure them that 'the people who matter know what you did'. Even if that's actually true at the time, those people will forget or move on, and in a couple of years the only thing anyone will remember is what's in the official history. To be absolutely sure, you can't beat writing the official history.*

feigned modesty · 'Oh, I didn't do much. I just helped out at one or two points.' The skill here is to sound sincere, while at the same time making it clear to your audience that you're just being typically modest. Obviously you had a bigger role than that, but you don't like to say.

---

* As Winston Churchill told Parliament in 1948, 'it will be found much better by all parties to leave the past to history, especially as I propose to write that history myself.'

presence · there's nothing like being in the office when things have gone well. And that means the right office. Michael Lewis's Wall Street memoir *Liar's Poker* describes an opportunist who took a Concorde flight to their bank's headquarters in New York to ensure he got the credit for a deal Lewis had set up in London.

narrative · People like to have stories about success and failure, which show that these things are about more than dumb chance. Journalists are looking for a hero or villain around whom they can build their story. Politicians, who one day hope to be Great Leaders, are predisposed to believe in the existence of such figures. Sport needs its mythic figures, whether they're players or managers. Business has looked on jealously and created its own hero executives. With alarming regularity, these are the same people who later turn out to have been running their companies into the ground, either by fraud or incompetence.

If Fred Goodwin can get a knighthood and a yacht for actions that nearly crashed the economy, there's absolutely no reason you can't get a pat on the back for a genuinely good idea that your colleague had while you were getting coffee.

Avoiding the Blame

It was said of Tony Blair that he was so bad at breaking bad news that he once ended up promoting someone he was supposed to be firing.* In order to avoid this sort of problem, and also out of cowardice, the modern management convention is that bad news should be broken by someone who doesn't have the power to alter the decision.

If you have to do bad-news breaking yourself, this is precisely the position you should take. Your refrain should be: 'It's not up to me, it's John's decision.' John should be inaccessible – on another continent, if not actually in a Trappist order. John hates personal approaches, so the victim's only route of access to him is through you. In fact, you can't even go to John yourself. You have to go through Bob. And Bob's terrified of John. So basically, you're just there to deliver the news and agree that it sucks.

Even if you're in the unfortunate position that it is your decision, there's no need to let on. You should still blame John. In fact, it's not even clear that John

---

* Although I've been unable to confirm this incident, a comment from Blair in his memoirs lends weight to it: 'It was always odd to be described as having this incredibly ruthless machine, when actually we had plenty of ruth; indeed, on occasions far too much of it.'

need exist. He's inaccessible anyway, so it's not as though his existence matters.

This technique – let's call it glove-puppetry – goes far beyond firing people or cancelling contracts. A popular British glove puppet is the Health and Safety Executive. This body, which exerts tyrannical control over the UK with its insistence that people should wear hard hats on construction sites and that open manholes should be clearly marked, is your ideal alibi for not doing whatever it is you don't want to do.

Recent examples include a council using health and safety laws to justify its refusal to clean up dog turds in a playground, a cafe citing them as a reason not to put toppings on ice cream, and a school ban on yo-yos.* If you don't want to get out of bed tomorrow, they're your best excuse.

How to Win at Twitter

If you wish to be seen as influential in the modern world, consider having a large Twitter following. Something about the way that the words appear on a screen means people believe things that have been

---

* These examples are all confirmed by the Health and Safety Executive's 'myth-busting' panel, along with a reported ban on people wearing flip-flops at work.

UNPLEDGES

Never underestimate the possibilities from a pledge. World leaders rarely visit each other without committing to double mutual trade over the next twenty years. When making such announcements, they're sure to mention the large amounts of money and jobs that will be generated by the 'deal'. They're not dissuaded by the fact that this promise to double a number that no one knows is beyond their control, and is dated long after they'll have left office. Indeed, the fact that these pledges will be forgotten long before they fall due is a large part of their appeal. You can do the same, and reap similar goodwill right now for making a promise that no one will remember or expect you to keep, the equivalent of promising that you'll be able to fit into your wedding outfit on your fortieth anniversary.

The three most common unpledges are:

1. **I'll call you:** I have already deleted you from my phone and blocked your number. But thanks for your help.

2. **we must have lunch:** we won't have lunch. Even if we both find ourselves alone in the same restaurant, I'll be at my own table.

3. **we must have coffee:** you're so repellent to me that I can't even bring myself to make an imaginary commitment to lunch.

tweeted without feeling the need to verify them. Take Graham Linehan, a writer of TV comedies, who, hours after the 2011 killing of Osama bin Laden, started a successful rumour that the al-Qaeda leader had been a fan of one of his shows, *The IT Crowd*.*

But how to get a big following? Obviously such things can be bought, but that seems a tawdry way to advance oneself. Much better to build an audience by being wise, funny and first with the news.

If by some unfortunate chance you aren't any of these things, you'll have to borrow from people who are. Simply take their smarts as your own. Not by plagiarism, but by 'commenting' on good tweets. As follows:

RT · inserted at the start of a tweet, this gives you ownership while looking as though you don't mean to steal the tweet but can't work out how to operate Twitter. Less convincing if you have to edit it to make it fit.

this · along with '+1', 'must read', 'what he said', 'brilliant', '*claps*', and 'yes', offer a way to justify your tweet-borrowage by 'adding value'. In this

---

* The next day, Linehan explained he'd been misled: the video footage from Pakistan actually showed bin Laden watching *The Big Bang Theory*.

case, the value you're adding is saying that this retweet, at least, implies endorsement.

interesting · most of the stuff you link to isn't, but this apparently is. Also dresses up as thoughtful scepticism your inability to say whether what you're pointing to is true.

hilarious · no scepticism here, just a reminder that you're the kind of perceptive person who can spot that a funny thing posted by someone else is indeed funny.

wow · all-purpose comment that is just as meaningful as the abbreviated '!'. It's definitely either a good thing, a bad thing, a stupid thing or a funny thing. But probably not a sad thing, because that's ...

just awful · add value by explaining your own reaction to the story of the toddlers drowning with the puppies. Or try 'so sad' or 'terrible news'.

via · advanced Twitter theft involves rewriting someone else's tweet, and then appearing polite by acknowledging your source at the end with a cheeky 'via ...' Really advanced theft involves two tweets: the first ripping off the original without any acknowledgement, and the second adding 'that last via ...'

big shock, if confirmed · typically appended to a brief tweet from a news organisation along the lines of 'WHITE HOUSE: PRESIDENT WOUNDED AFTER SHOTS FIRED AT MOTOR-CADE'. Both parts are essential to really Add Value – while quite a few people might share the 'big shock' insight, 'if confirmed' is the caveat that puts you in a special category. After all, if it's not confirmed, it won't be a big shock. You can't buy that kind of wisdom.

Questions for group discussion

1. *Most people who've dealt with you think of you as a pretty straight sort of guy. How can you keep your image fresh?*
   a) *two or three eye-catching initiatives with which you can be personally associated*
   b) *only go one way, and do not deploy a reverse gear.*

2. *How late in a tweet is it acceptable to credit someone whose idea or joke you have stolen? Is it enough to credit them on the same day?*

5. POLITICAL UNCOMMUNICATIONS

While politics draws in many other areas of uncommunication, it has some niches all its own. Only politicians are these days expected to make persuasive speeches, and only they are allowed to take money off the public without selling them something first. Front-rank politicians live under constant scrutiny. They are expected to be interesting and engaging without ever being controversial, to be exceptional and yet normal, to run the country without losing the common touch. It will be no surprise, then, that the best communicators are often the best uncommunicators, too.

In this chapter, you will learn:
- How to Give a Political Speech
- How to Demand an Inquiry
- How to Make an Unpromise
- Whom to Tax

Friends, Romans, Countrymen

The job of the political speech is to provide safe packaging for your news announcement. No one will read it, and most of your audience will lose concentration after the first five minutes. What's more, the modern method of news management is to brief the most important bits of the speech to the press the night before anyway, so any of your audience who care about your announcement will have read all about it. You do still have to give the speech anyway. (Expert tip: if the announcement hasn't been as well received as you expected, you still have time to adjust it, and then insert the words 'contrary to what you may have read ...' into the speech.)

If you're about to say something that hasn't been briefed, but which you'd like people to report, preface it with 'this may be a bit controversial', to wake the journalists up.

So the bulk of the speech is the rhetorical equivalent of polystyrene chippings: a bit of mischaracterising your opponents, some flattering of your audience, a topical joke or two. Anything to get you above fifteen minutes. If you just stand up and say you've decided to run for president, people won't feel they've had their money's worth. Ask Abraham Lincoln. The Gettysburg Address is under

300 words long, took less than five minutes to give, and yet not only paid tribute to the dead of the battle but also argued that the American Civil War was the summit of mankind's historic struggle for freedom and democracy. The *London Times* pronounced it 'dull' and said it rendered the event 'ludicrous'. The *Chicago Times* said it was embarassing and 'dishwattery'[sic].

They'd probably have preferred something like this:

> Thank you all so much for that welcome. I want to tell you how much I appreciate the fantastic work that happens here.[1] It's so important. Thank you for all that you do.
>
> I won't take up too much of your valuable time, but I just want to share some thoughts with you about one of the big debates going on in politics right now.
>
> It's about straw men.
>
> Now I know I'll have lost some of you right there, but stay with me, because straw men are vital to the way we conduct ourselves as a country. They go right to the core of how we do our politics.
>
> There are some people who say that straw men are the answer to everything.[2]
>
> And there are other people who say that straw men are actually the whole problem.[3]

---

[1] *Whatever it is. I have a note here somewhere.*

[2] *No there aren't.*

[3] *Not really any of them, either.*

I don't take either of those views. I certainly think that straw men can be a distraction, as when they're used in speeches by my opponent.

But I also think they can be extremely valuable, for instance when I use them in my own speeches.

So to people who say to me:[4] 'Stop now, and never use a rhetorical device in a speech again!'

I say: 'I'm sorry, but I just can't agree with you.'

I'm an old-fashioned member of my party,[5] and I'm proud[6] of what we've done in government for rhetorical devices. There's nothing in my party's traditions about suppressing empty rhetoric.[7]

And that includes straw men.

You know, as a parent of young children,[8] I often find myself thinking about the dingle dangle scarecrow.

Let me share his story with you.

When all the cows were sleeping.

And the sun had gone to bed.

Up jumped the scarecrow.

And – and I think this is really important – this is what he said.

I'm a dingle, dangle scarecrow.

With a flippy floppy hat.

---

[4] They don't.

[5] I'm not, which is why they elected me leader. And also why they don't really trust me.

[6] Use of 'proud' is directly proportional to the extent people tell me I should be ashamed.

[7] Though if I'm honest there's a chunk of people in my party who could be persuaded to ban just about anything.

[8] I have a note of their names in my wallet.

You know, the dingle dangle scarecrow didn't want much. Just to shake his hands like this. And shake his feet like that. But who will speak for him? Not our opponents, I'm afraid. They've shown this week that they're far more interested in standing up for the big Wicker Men than they are for the humble dingle dangle scarecrow.

It's increasingly clear to me that the real divide in politics isn't between those who use straw men and those who don't.

It's between those who want empty words, and those who say no. No, we demand more. We demand full words.

I know which side I'm on. And I think you know which side you're on, too.

This isn't the time to give in to fear and hate, as some will tell you.[9] This is the moment we must reach out to our friends, neighbours and fellow citizens and speak of the world we want our children to grow up in.

To me, the great test of who we are as a society is how we treat our scarecrows.

I dream of a world where we can all shake our hands like this.

And shake our feet like that.

Will you join me in daring to dream that dream? To hope that hope?

Together, we can build that country.

Thank you very much. Now, I think we've got time for some questions from our friends in the media.[10]

---

[9] *Direct rebuke to those people who are saying: 'This is the perfect moment to give into fear and hate.'*

[10] *Note to self: mustn't sound so sarcastic when I say 'friends'.*

Will It Be on Oath?

Out of power is one of the most frustrating places for a politician to be. Fundamentally, it's governments that set the agenda: they introduce the legislation, spend the money and deploy the troops. If you find yourself in opposition, the best you can hope to achieve, at least at first, is to make life difficult for the government, through guerrilla warfare. A great way to achieve this is to force them to hold an inquiry. Not an internal inquiry of the sit-around-for-two-months-and-then-announce-everything-is-fine variety (the only sort you should ever agree to if you're in charge), a proper, no-holds-barred, public inquiry, of the sort that could turn up all manner of problems.

The best thing about calling for an inquiry is that it's superficially so appealing: who could be against finding out more facts? It'd be like being against science. You can emphasise this point by saying that the inquiry is essential to ensure that we 'learn lessons'.

The kind of inquiry you call for should be:

full · as opposed to 'not full'.

independent · naturally, the government will try to manipulate the findings of any inquiry to which it is too close. Or it will if it's halfway competent.

judge-led · quite why it's so important to pick an elderly gentleman from the upper reaches of the establishment is a mystery. But this is a vital part of the invocation. You should then express utmost faith in the judge, whom you will assert to be a valiant fighter for justice and inquirer after truth, all the way through the process. Until he clears the government of wrongdoing, at which stage you should mutter that the government knew what it was doing when it appointed him.

on oath · your point here is that the members of the government under inquiry are so untrustworthy that they're bound to lie unless they're made to specifically promise not to. A promise they'll keep, because no one has ever lied in court.

What you don't need to know is what question the inquiry is supposed to investigate. If challenged on this, the answer is always the same: **who knew what, and when.**

It is possible to overdo it. Between 2010 and 2012, the British Labour Party called for at least ten public inquiries, including some they appeared not to be aware they'd demanded.* They eased off after this was pointed out.

---

*   A study of the party's press releases suggests these were: school buildings; care homes; breast implants; the 2011 riots; phone-hacking; border security; political lobbying; banking; school exams; railway companies.

Political Uncomms

There are some words that have a special meaning in the mouth of a politician. Whether you utter them yourself, or simply have to listen to them, you should know what they are.

boldness, clarity and purpose · what we stand for. Our opponents stand for timidity, opacity and lack of direction.

bribe · an attractive offer to the electorate made by our opponent.

coalition · an organisation with a fundamental internal split. Or an organisation that only represents one viewpoint, but wishes to appear broad-minded.

consultation · we know what we want to do, and we're not going to let the fact that we can't work out how to do it stop us from announcing it.

democratic · when it appears in a country's name: 'totalitarian'. As in the German Democratic Republic, the Democratic People's Republic of Korea and the Democratic Republic of the Congo.

extended readiness · an excellent phrase we devised for the British government, who were looking for a nicer way to say that when their new Queen Elizabeth aircraft carrier was complete, it was going to be put into storage for a while to save money.

hard-hitting · the kind of speech that you'll be making.

liberal metropolitan elite · this is, apparently, how yokels refer to the people they used to call 'city folk'.

middle class · everyone thinks they're middle class, just as they all think their children are 'above average'. Anything that can be described as helping middle-class people with above-average children is a sure-fire hit.

more widely · where we need to look for answers, because we don't like the ones we've found in the places we've looked so far.

petition · once a way of demonstrating to power that you had mass support for your argument, these now serve one of two purposes: first, to reveal either that ten thousand people care enough about an issue to click on a web link; and second, to allow political parties to gather the email addresses of likely supporters.

playing politics · an irregular verb, conjugated as follows: I am raising an important issue, you are scoring points, he is playing politics.

profits · these are a good thing when a company makes them, unless it makes too many of them, or makes them from selling things that people really need, like healthcare, in which case they're a bad thing.

projecting force · invading or bombing.

public diplomacy · propaganda.

raising awareness · moaning, when done by a worthy pressure group.

reform · what we support, as the solution to all problems.

regime · government for which I didn't vote. Or for which I did vote, but with which I now disagree.

send a message · the justification for any measure that is going to fail in its stated aim, but will nonetheless be popular with voters. It may also, apparently, 'show that we're serious'.

the right balance · what my proposal strikes.

the usual way · the manner in which this decision will be made, once you stop asking difficult questions.

this is what we'd do if we were in government right now · an excellent political tactic for opposition parties far from an election is to call on the government to do nice things and then complain when it doesn't. When, inevitably, you're challenged as to whether you're making a policy commitment for your own party, this is the answer you can give. Because, in an uncertain world, the one thing that absolutely isn't going to happen is you finding yourself in government right now.

we will implement the inquiry's main recommendations · having first decided to ignore the ones we don't like.

UNPROMISING

There are three levels of political promise:

1. **aspiration:** something we'd like to do, but won't.

2. **pledge:** something we'll promise to do, but won't.

3. **unpromise:** something you'll think we've promised to do, until we explain why this just shows you weren't paying attention.

A good example of an unpromise was the one offered in 2005 by the British Labour Party of a referendum on the European Constitution. The party never mentioned that this line, which enabled them to shut down a difficult subject during that year's election, hung on the constitution surviving a series of other tricky referendums in other countries, which it was unlikely to do, and didn't.

Tax Has to Be Taxing

Roads, hospitals, police and schools all need to be paid for. The ideal people to tax are easy to identify:

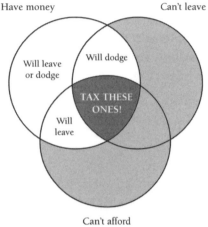

There's a limit to how much you can raise from people who don't have any money. And people with millions can move it, or themselves, out of your reach faster than you can chase. So the people you want to tax are those who have some money, can't leave the country, and can't afford to dodge you. Happily, in an advanced economy, there are plenty of these people, and they're generally fairly easily fooled.

Don't Call It Tax

Officially, Britain has three income tax rates: the basic rate of 20 per cent, the higher rate of 40 per cent, and the additional rate of 45 per cent. This is kept simple by saying that another tax, National Insurance, isn't income tax. Even though it's paid on income, and for someone on median earnings will represent nearly half the direct tax they pay.

At the top of the scale, an extra 20 per cent is added to the income tax rate by the innocent-sounding 'reduced personal allowance'.

If you include these extras, the tax paid on income as your earnings rise starts at 12 per cent, moves to 32 per cent, then 42 per cent, then 62 per cent, then 42 per cent and then 47 per cent. But try finding those numbers in a Treasury publication.

Don't Call Tax Cuts Bribes

The spirit of government austerity requires that people shouldn't feel like they're being bribed. But they should definitely feel they're getting something. In Britain, the coalition government that took office in 2010 hit this perfectly with one of its most famous and popular policies, raising the starting level of tax. It was apparently simple – 'you pay no tax on the first £10,500 you earn' (which relied on saying National Insurance wasn't a tax) – and was always described as a tax cut for low earners. Actually, the households that benefitted most were ones with above-average incomes, as they tend to have two earners, and therefore enjoyed twice the allowance. A tax cut for your middle-class voters that everyone can pretend is mainly benefitting the 'working poor' is the ideal tax policy.

Talk About How You're Cutting It

You should aim to have a big headline cut, and then lots of little rises to get the money back. That income-tax cut from the coalition cost the government over £12 billion a year, according to the Institute for Fiscal Studies. In another part of the forest, one of the coalition's first acts was to increase Value-added Tax to 20 per cent. Which raised a little more than £12 billion a year.*

Pretend That Someone Else Will Pay

'I'm going to take cash off rich people and spend it on you' is obviously an attractive political pitch, but you do have to be a little bit careful: the voters aren't *that* stupid. However, carefully deployed, this can be effective. Take the Robin Hood Tax campaign, which

---

* Actually, because the VAT rise took effect immediately, and the income-tax cut arrived in stages, the net effect of these two changes was to raise money for the Treasury.

wants a levy on financial transactions. It describes this as 'a tiny tax' that will raise £20 billion a year. Only one of those propositions can be true.

Build a Time Machine to Get Money from the Future

For governments, such a time machine exists, and it's called the bond market. Politicians often talk about running the government like a household, but the difference between you and the government is that you will one day stop working and die. This will make people reluctant to lend you money as you get older and they start to wonder about their chances of getting it back. Governments, on the other hand, hope to continue overseeing growing economies until the end of time. That means they can generally find people willing to lend them money on the promise of being paid back decades hence. So if you want to spend more than you can raise in tax, simply run a deficit and borrow the difference. There are excellent reasons for doing this:

1. It's much easier to get the guy who's doing your job in twenty years to collect the money from people who're paying tax in twenty years than it is for you to collect the money from people who're paying tax right now. Well, it's easier for you.

2. The guy who was doing your job twenty years ago did it to you, so why not 'pay it forward'?
3. Inflation and the fact that the economy will have grown means it should be easier to pay the money back in twenty years than it would be now.
4. What could go wrong?

Questions for group discussion

Your message to the people of this country at the next election is:

a) *Kinder, Gentler Nation*
b) *Reform, Prosperity and Peace*
c) *It's Time for Action*
d) *Change That Works for You*
e) *Freedom, Justice, Honesty*
f) *Change You Can Believe In*
g) *It's Time for Common Sense*
h) *A Future Fair for All*
i) *Forward, Not Back*
j) *Prosperity and Progress*
k) *Forward*
l) *In Your Heart, You Know We're Right*

6. UNEARNING YOUR KEEP

Uncommunication lends itself well to the business of selling, easing people's money out of their pocket and into yours. Deploy conveniently imprecise language to bridge the gap between what people want and what you're offering. As we'll show you, there are lines of work that depend heavily on the customer not understanding what it is that they're actually being sold.

In this chapter, you will learn about:
➠ Unreal Estate
➠ Empty Words
➠ Unendorsement
➠ Fund Unmanagement
➠ Forecasting
➠ Self-Unhelp

Unreal Estate

Those who feel they would like to practise deception at a low level before progressing to its heights should consider selling houses. Estate agents are bound by law not to lie, of course, but they have the distinct advantage that no one really expects them to tell the truth, so the slightest nod towards accuracy will impress customers with your honest and upright character. Then it only remains to write up the property details.

back on the market · we really thought we'd finally shifted this one. Who knew that blind people still have a sense of smell?

bordering · a 15-minute walk from somewhere you might actually want to live.

conveniently located · opposite a pub, over a bookies, next to a takeaway.

cosy · you'll lose the remote control during the move, but discover you can reach the TV from the sofa anyway.

deceptively ... · brace yourself, the next word is going to be a lie.

easy-to-maintain living space · with a little effort, you can touch all the walls of the lounge at once.

excellent transport links · you can see the motorway from the front door, and the high-speed rail line from the kitchen.

four bedrooms · only kidding. Three bedrooms and a room in which a single bed would fit. Vertically.

garden flat · basement flat.

ideal buy-to-let investment · you wouldn't want to actually live in it yourself.

in need of some updating and offered with no onward chain · occupied by a widow and a series of cats from 1978 until last month, when someone noticed the smell, and the police found the bits of her body that the cats had left.

low-maintenance rear garden · eight paving slabs and something in a pot that we'll be calling a rhododendron.

many character features · when you flush the upstairs toilet, all the lights flicker.

needs modernisation · needs modernisation to get it to the mid 80s. To get it to the twenty-first century, you'd be best advised to burn it to the ground and start again.

open day · we saw *The Hunger Games*, and we thought that we could probably sell flats that way, too.

purpose-built residential development · to distinguish it from the housing estate two miles away that was intended as a shopping mall.

reduced · we told them eight months ago that if they wanted to get what the people up the road got, they'd need to put a door on the bathroom, but would they listen?

stamp duty exempt area · things are so bad round here, the government has intervened.

superb · ordinary.

viewing recommended · unlike the next property in the list, which is most likely to be sold to someone who hasn't visited it.

well appointed · actually, we don't know what this means either, but we put it in all the time, and no one's ever asked.

within easy reach of local schools · the traffic jam outside the house clears just after 9.30 each morning.

would benefit from · lacks.

would suit DIY enthusiast · our ideal buyer has a high opinion of his own ability to overcome the impossible, and will electrocute himself within six months.

would suit professional couple · no scum need enquire.

Empty Words

If estate agency whets your appetite for selling, there's more money and better clothes in writing advertising copy. The trick here is to achieve a fluent emptiness, to write smooth sentences that seem to promise the earth but in reality commit to nothing.

Look at a car brochure: it doesn't just have a rev counter, it has 'sophisticated technology'. Its interior is 'exquisitely detailed'. It has 'components', not parts. And they weren't made, they were 'engineered'.

At the other end of the scale, look at a beer can. To taste it, Heineken is a fairly average mass-produced fizzy beer. But look at the label: 'Premium Lager', made to an 'Original Recipe'.

Any of the following words can be dropped into sentences without making more than the vaguest hint of a pledge.

contoured · this product exists in three dimensions.

convenient · not inconvenient.

custom-fitted · having measured both the thing that this was supposed to fit, and this thing, the numbers were pretty close.

cutting edge · now some distance behind 'bleeding edge'.

designer · twice as expensive as the apparently identical thing next to it.

durable · it won't fall apart before you get home.

dynamic · we'd like you to think that wearing this shirt will make you look like a go-getter.

easy-to-clean · you can wipe it.

elegant · not provably ugly.

enhanced · this bit means we can charge more for it.

WOULD THEY LIE TO YOU?

finish · it's finished.

flexible · bendy.

fluid · typically used of things that would more accurately be described as 'solid'.

helps protect · but doesn't, in itself, protect.

high-grade · there exist on the planet worse materials than the ones we've used.

high-quality · relative to some of the crap that's out there, this thing is quite good.

iconic · we're particularly proud of this thing.

long-lasting · this will last a length of time.

natural · made from things that occur somewhere in the universe.

next generation · this generation.

power · this car has an engine. The engine makes it go in a way that conforms to Newton's Second Law of Motion.

precision · as opposed to imprecision.

robust · you can drop it. But probably not onto concrete.

sculpted · this device is the shape we intended it to be.

seamlessly · no needles or threads were deployed at any stage in the making of this mobile phone.

select · there was a process of selection to get this into the box. It didn't just fall in while our backs were turned.

A TOUCH OF CLASS

If you'd like to charge a bit more for whatever product you're selling, try writing one (or more) of these words on the packet:

artisan	**finest**
bespoke	**gourmet**
best	**premium**
bijou	**masterpiece**

snug · it fits.

state of the art · we made this tablet computer in the way these things are made these days, rather than the way they would have made them in the nineteenth century. Although nineteenth-century factory owners would recognise the employment contracts and indeed rates of pay of the people who made it.

stylish · we toyed with making something that was desperately out of fashion, and decided instead to make something that will be desperately out of fashion next year.

sustainable · I think we'll be able to keep this up for quite a while.

tough · not actually flimsy.

value · hey, cheapskates, this is the one you're

looking for. But you should know we're all laugh-
ing at you when you buy it.

world-class · this exists in the world.

Unendorsements

As you move to higher-level marketing, you'll discover that you don't sell things by telling people how
good they are. Steve Jobs, a black-belt uncommunicator, noted that successful advertising doesn't focus
on a product's merits. Instead it tries to associate
the item with attractive ideas and people.* He made
the observation in 1997 as he revealed a new TV ad
for Apple, which, in his words, 'honoured' figures
including Einstein, Gandhi, Martin Luther King and
John Lennon by using them to sell computers. Jobs
did note that many of those featured weren't alive or
indeed famous technology users, but he explained
that 'we know that if they'd ever used a computer, it
would have been a Mac.'

Here are some of the other things that Lennon,
who before his death was noted for urging listeners

---

* Not everyone agrees. As he was becoming a star, Justin Bieber
offered to be a 'brand ambassador' for Blackberry in return
for $200,000 and twenty of the smartphones. The company
turned him down. This would be the stand-out catastrophic
mistake for Research In Motion, the phone's makers, were it
not for the intense competition.

to 'imagine no possessions', has been used to sell since he passed on:

Bavaria Beer
Citroën DS3 hatchback
One Laptop per Child
The VW Golf
The Anti-Defamation League
Allan Gray Investments
One2One mobile phones
Adlens glasses
Epiphone guitars
Nike
Ben & Jerry's ice cream
Cisco Systems Computer Networking Technology
Banco Itaú
J. C. Penney

The field is therefore open to have any dead person endorse anything. Stand by for Abraham Lincoln selling Gillette razors, Winston Churchill advertising Weight Watchers, and Pope John Paul II endorsing Durex.

False Reports

It isn't just marketeers who have to dress up reality. When even the Education Secretary tells

Parliament that he wants all schoolchildren to be above average,* teachers can be forgiven for thinking that they'll never keep everyone happy. The incentives to gloss over the truth about your children are strong, so we'll have to forgive teachers a little bit of euphemism when it comes to school reports.**

a natural leader · we can't prove that she organised the Year 11 Christmas trip to the pub, but you should know that we know it was her.

eager to please · I've nothing against a little bit of crawling, but even I think he's an obsequious little toad.

energises others · has to sit in a separate area of the classroom or no one gets any work done.

engaging, popular and lively member of the class · never shuts up.

---

* This seems to be a reference to Michael Gove, who in 2012 explained this would be possible by 'getting better all the time'. Asked whether, as a child, he had been 'better at literacy than numeracy', the minister replied: 'I cannot remember.'

** This can create problems. In his book *The British Dream*, David Goodhart describes how Turkish immigrants to the UK failed to realise that their children's reports were written in a code where 'satisfactory' meant 'unsatisfactory', and so were taken by surprise when they failed their exams.

flair for drama · will burst into tears mid-lesson at the drop of a hat.

gift for computers · we've tried everything to stop him downloading pornography on the school network, and he keeps beating us.

good communication skills · we can't get a word in.

good progress · she's started turning up.

imaginative · we have no idea whether anything she says is true.

improving · he was terrible at this. Now he's merely awful.

keen to share his knowledge with the class · I honestly don't blame the rest of them for flushing his head down the toilets.

shows leadership potential · pushes classes into anarchy in seconds.

tries hard · his problem isn't lack of effort. It's lack of ability.

unique sense of humour · wildly inappropriate sense of humour.

vivacious personality · her skirt's too short.

vivid imagination · inventive liar.

well-mannered · I have no memory of your son whatsoever. Is he in my class?

working towards · can't do it, won't ever do it.

Fund Unmanagement

Every now and then Hollywood tells us a tale of an evil financier getting rich with a Wall Street scam. One might very well feel tempted by the prospect of making a million dollars a week, but worried about the possibility of losing it all and going to prison. Happily, it's perfectly possible to take large amounts of money off people completely legally. Just become a fund manager.

Fund managers are the people who make bets on the stock market with other people's savings and pension funds. To compensate them for the inconvenience of this, they take a small percentage of your savings – just a couple of per cent. But it's a small percentage of a big number: in 2013 there was around £750 billion invested in British funds alone. A couple of per cent of that covers a few lunches.

You don't need to be any good at managing funds. Very few of those who do it make enough back for their customers to cover their fees. People will just assume you must be all right, because of Regulation, Competition, and Graphs.

Regulation

This is the way we describe a situation in which a small group of government staff too slow or scrupulous to make it in the private sector are outwitted by a large number of expensive lawyers. The world believes that the purpose of financial regulation is to prevent people from being swindled. In fact, the purpose of financial regulation is to ensure that people are only swindled by government-approved means.

As a general rule, regulators are usually only interested in preventing fraud. Greed or incompetence are beyond their remit. This means you can be as useless as you like, and charge as much as you can get away with, so long as you don't actually lie about it.

Competition

In theory, poor fund managers would be weeded out by the free market, with angry customers moving their money elsewhere. This is indeed the argument you should offer whenever someone suggests tighter regulation. And when customers understand what they're buying, the free market does indeed work very well. It's why supermarkets don't poison their customers very often. Happily for fund managers, this condition isn't met when it comes to investing. Study after study shows that the best funds to invest in are those that track the market, do little trading and charge low fees. But still funds that trade a lot, charge high fees and underperform flourish. Indeed, one study found that as funds' performance gets worse, they increase their fees – the customers that stay obviously don't care they're being overcharged, so you might as well keep their money.*

Graphs

The reason you'll persuade people to let you take a slice of their savings every year is that you won't put it like that. You'll use words like 'actively managed', 'profit-hunting', 'boutique', 'growth' and 'opportunity'. If you want to charge a lot more, you can call yourself a 'hedge fund'.

And you'll use graphs to make your point. You'll have a graph on your brochure that shows that for the last three years your fund has outperformed those cheap passive funds. People will know they can trust your graph, because your graph is regulated. The regulators will check that, out of the twenty funds you set up, the one you've decided to put on the front of your brochure did indeed, for the time period you chose, do what you said it did. And they won't say a word about what happened to it

---

* Studies suggest that this is also the reason Nigerian email scams are so obvious: it saves the scammers time by ensuring that only *really* gullible people reply.

just before then, or what the rest of your funds did, because their main concern will be making sure that somewhere in very small letters, your brochure points out that when it comes to fund managers, there's no reliable link between past and future performance.

You should also use the following phrases:

dead cat bounce · any rise in the market following a fall, if you didn't predict it.

enhanced indexing · an index tracker which has to charge more to pay for all its advertising.

proprietary strategy · the way that a fund that doesn't track the market justifies charging you more to produce lower returns.

seeking alpha · a term that means you try to make money when the market is falling. Or, as you'll put it, you 'aim to seek maximum return in all market conditions'. Unlike the lesser fund managers, who by implication sometimes deliberately set out to lose money.

unlock · a more exciting way of describing the process of spending your retirement savings early.

If asked to justify why the market isn't performing as you said it would, you need only two answers:

profit-taking · I think it should be going up, but for reasons I don't understand, it's going down.

bargain-hunting · I think it should be going down, but for reasons I don't understand, it's going up.

Crystal Balls

There are two ways to make your living predicting the future. One is to call yourself 'Madame Savary', join the circus and sell yourself as a Tarot reader. The other is to get an economics PhD and go and work on Wall Street. The first one has lower start-up costs, but the second one pays much better, and involves less elephant dung. For a fortune-teller, the clientele is the desperate, the gullible and the lovelorn. For an economic forecaster, it's banks, the government and the public.

You may at this point object that you don't know how to predict the future. Fortunately, neither does anyone else.

The measure of the size of a country's economy is its gross domestic product. The technique for forecasting it is quite straightforward: if things are going normally, say that it'll be what it normally is. If everyone seems a bit nervous, say a bit less. If they seem optimistic, a bit more. Drop in a selection of the following phrases: 'our model for the economy', 'seeing strong growth in construction', 'manufacturing output', 'confidence' and 'animal spirits'.

Worried you'll be caught out? Let's look at how bad everyone else is. In April 2007, the British Treasury published forty-four economic predictions from different bodies. Just one saw trouble ahead. In April 2008, it was still one out of forty-four predicting recession, even though by this stage, the question wasn't so much seeing the future as looking out of the window: Britain had already had the first bank run for more than a century and was actually entering recession at that moment. By April 2009, the forecasters had caught up, and predicted a recession in 2009. But there were only forty of them. Other institutions, most notably Lehman Bros, had disappeared from the list – something else they hadn't foreseen.

Economic forecasters might point out that they do better during more normal times of steady growth, but this is like a seismologist saying they're better at predicting when there won't be earthquakes than when there will: it's not a lot of use.

GUESSING GAMES

There are five kinds of forecast you can offer:

1. **The obvious prediction:** it will be colder in the winter than in the summer.

2. **The consensus prediction:** the same guess everyone else is making.

3. **The wishful prediction:** the guess based on what your audience hopes will happen.

4. **The original, counter-intuitive prediction:** based on the realisation that most people have misread the current situation.

5. **The original, counter-intuitive guess:** based on the realisation that these make you look smart if you're right, and that people generally don't remember when you get it wrong.

How Shall I Fire Thee? Let Me Count the Ways

As you rise through industry, you will periodically have to fire large numbers of staff in order to keep your own job. This shouldn't cause you to lose sleep – it's simply the natural order of things. But don't call it 'mass lay-offs' – not when you can call it something less blunt:

career opportunity · we're giving you one of these, but elsewhere. Because what we're doing to you here is firing you.

de-layering · job cuts.

democratic streamlining · job cuts.

employment separations · job cuts.

equalisation of the payroll to manpower requirement · job cuts.

organisational realignment · job cuts.

our staff are our greatest asset · we're about to announce job cuts.

resigned by mutual agreement · fired.

restructuring · job cuts.

shaping up for tomorrow · by firing people today.

there will be job losses · you will be fired.

unfortunate depreciation of our greatest asset · job cuts.

CASE STUDY: OUR NUMBER ONE PRIORITY

Amazon, responding to the annual round of Christmas undercover investigations into work conditions in its distribution centres, said in 2013 that the safety of staff was 'our number one priority'. Amazon has a fantastic reputation for price, reliability, customer service and innovation. But apparently the one area where it persistently gets a really terrible press is its 'number one priority'. That must be frustrating.

I Can Make You Slightly Poorer

Although we were initially inclined to sneer, some former students have made vast fortunes from self-help books. Writing them, that is, not reading them. These works are the modern world's answer to the indulgences sold by the medieval church. People buy them in the hope that they'll wash their sins away, or at the very least remove the evidence of their gluttony. Get it right, and there is actually no limit to the number you can sell. You will need:

a hope · flatter stomach, tighter abs, greater wealth, a better marriage, perter breasts.

a gimmick · the broccoli purée diet; letting your inner fox eat your inner rabbit; fifteen minutes of crunches before bed; an obscure Old Testament prayer.

a tale · I used to be just like you: fat, poor, unhappy and saggy. Then I heard about this miracle technique from a friend. I didn't believe it (I'm not a sap, and neither are you, despite your having bought my book), but I decided to investigate. I was amazed by what I discovered. Now I'm fulfilled and rich. And 'energised' – you wouldn't believe how 'energised' I am.

a science bit · don't worry, we're not talking about peer-reviewed, double-blind studies here. You just need something plausible, ideally mixing ancient South American wisdom with words like 'alkaloids' or 'polypeptides'. Feel free to mention that 'science can't explain why this works' – your readers can't explain how their car works, and they're pretty sure that doesn't make them dumb.

a promise · stick with me for thirty days, and you'll get your desires. Thirty days is about right: no one can stick to anything for a month, especially not in January, which is when all the world's self-help books are consumed. When it doesn't work, they'll blame themselves. And if by some chance they do manage to stick to the programme, it's pretty unlikely they'll be able to do lasting physical damage in that time.

formatting · you'll want to break up the text with short sentences.

Really.

Short.

Sentences.

Some of them in italic.

Some of them in bold.

And some of them in bold italic.

filler · recipes, exercises, mantras, a pretend map of the brain – take your pick. This is the stuff that gets the book from 30 pages to 250. Sadly, you need quite a lot of it. Happily, no one will read it, as they'll put the book down on day eight and never touch it again. Your market isn't people with self-discipline.

Questions for group discussion:

1. *Which is the most effective way to fire staff?*
   a) *deactivating their security passes before they arrive at work*
   b) *inviting them onto a conference call, and then telling them that if they can hear you, they don't have a job*
   c) *issuing a press release about their firing, and letting a journalist tell them*
   d) *posting a message on their Facebook page.*

2. *Which of these marketing campaigns would you be most proud to be associated with?*
   a) *offering $25,000 Mahatma Gandhi-branded fountain pens in Mumbai*
   b) *offering an Africa-themed burger in Europe during a famine in Africa.*

7. KEEPING UNCOUNT

We turn finally to statistics. What a friend we have in numbers. They impress into silence people otherwise confident in their arguments. A well-chosen statistic, placed before the public, can settle a debate.

You are helped by a general ignorance about anything that requires even a basic sum. Fortunately, those who intuitively grasp how numbers work have generally become so frustrated with the rest of humanity that they've given up correcting statistical errors. Their explanations are in any case generally tedious and jargon-heavy. You should take advantage of this if you find yourself in a debate with someone who's quoting numbers at you. Quote your own back, however unreliable they may be. Even if you find yourself 'fact-checked', the likeliest outcome is that the audience will conclude none of the numbers quoted in an argument can be trusted – neither yours nor your opponent's.

In this chapter, you will learn:

➡ Averages
➡ Percentages
➡ Big Numbers
➡ Small Numbers
➡ Graphs

I Don't Mean When You Think I Mean (I'm Using the Median)

We will start with the basic weapons in your armoury.

decimal places · there's something about a precise number that leaves the reader under the impression that it must be the result of precise thinking. Say that polls show 'about a third' of people support something, and you'll be giving an accurate assessment. Say '32.6 per cent', you'll sound like a scientist. It's important not to overdo this: one or two decimal places is usually the right number. Quote anything except pi to four decimal places, and people will start to have doubts about you.

average · a great little word, because people think they know what it means, but they don't. Probably they're thinking of the **mean** – the result of adding up all the values in a range, and dividing by the total number of values. But for lots of important statistics, including pay, the calculation more commonly used is the **median** – the result of arranging all the values in order and then picking the middle one. Statisticians like the median because it strips out extreme values and shows the middle point. You should ignore them and pick the one that best supports your case. If you want to argue that you're underpaid, you could point out that UK average annual pay in 2013 was £27,174 (the mean). If you want to counter-argue that someone is overpaid, simply reply that the average was £21,905 (the median). The Office for National Statistics will back you either way.

percentages · nothing lends authority like a percentage. And they come with an added bonus of a look of terror in the eyes of your audience, who know they're being confronted with Hard Science, but have no way to assess its reliability.

An under-noticed property of percentages is that they're bigger on the way up than they are on the way down.

If the price of something rises 100 per cent and then falls 50 per cent, it's back where it started. The practical application of that works like this:

'While it's true that under our management the value of your investment fell 23 per cent this year, you should keep in mind that it rose 28 per cent the year before.'

Translation: 'You gave us £1,000 to look after, and we turned it into £1,280 pounds last year, and then £986 this year. Now, let's talk about our fee.'

Percentages are a way of comparing two numbers: on their own they mean nothing. Thankfully, very few people grasp that. So let's say you're working out how much to pay your staff this year. Inflation is running at 3 per cent, but you don't want to match that. Take Janet, who earned £30,000 last year, with a £1,000 bonus. You call her in:

'Look, it's been a really tough year, and we're just going to have to hold basic salaries down across the board, so we're freezing everyone's pay. But I want you to know that I really appreciate the work you've done this year, so I've managed to get you 90 per cent of your bonus from last year. I'd be grateful if you kept that quiet – most people aren't getting that amount.'

Last year, Janet made £31,000. This year, just to keep up with inflation – for her money to buy as much as it did last year – she needs £31,930. You're giving her £30,000 in salary, and £900 in bonus – a total of £30,900. And you've made it sound generous.

big numbers · you can always impress with a big number. And you can always make a number big with a moment's thought. For a start, in government and any large business, most numbers you might want to talk about come with 'million' on the end. That makes them big right from the get-go. But you can make them bigger. Why not add up several years' worth of the number, to give you a figure 'over the term of this government' or 'over the decade'?

small numbers · is someone waving a big number at you? Cut them down to size with the miracle of division. Someone complaining you wasted £10 million of taxpayer's money on gin and crisps? Let's give that some perspective: the British government spends more than 650 billion pounds a year. The US federal government blows more than $3.5 trillion each year. In either country, you can refer to any public spending number that doesn't end in billion as 'basically a rounding error'. As an alternative, why not work out a per-person cost. The British royal family is always keen to point out that they cost less than a pound per taxpayer per year, which makes them sound very cheap, until you recall that there are 29 million British taxpayers, and rather fewer royals.

A Picture Obscures a Thousand Words

Graphs are a great way of conveying numbers clearly in a way that helps people understand them. And they're a tremendous way of conveying numbers in a way that stops people from understanding them.

Because you're drawing the graph, you get to choose what's shown, and how. We'll deal with how the numbers are shown first. Your audience will probably have learned to draw graphs in school, and will imagine they all look something like this line graph or this bar chart:

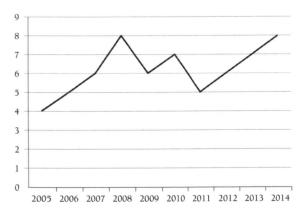

Things

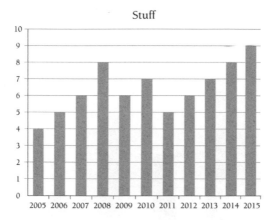

Note how the vertical axis goes all the way down to zero. Let's change that to make the chart look slightly more impressive:

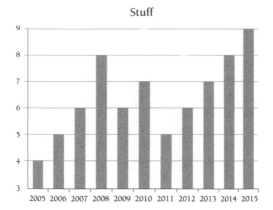

Now, do we want it to look as though stuff is getting worse?

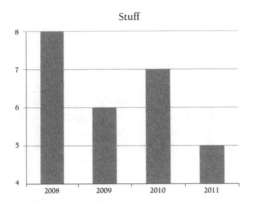

Or better?

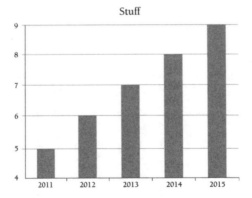

Let's see that in action, by looking at British employment data. Here's the last ten years:

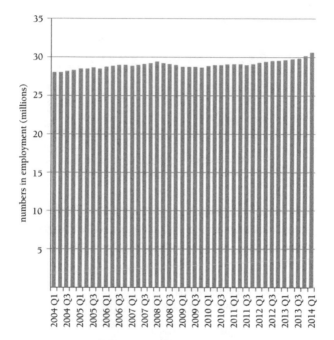

The British Conservative Party found a slightly more effective presentation of that data (overleaf).

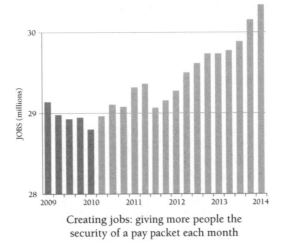

Creating jobs: giving more people the
security of a pay packet each month

Of course, both of these graphs have a scale. But there's
no actual obligation on you to do that. Take this graph
from a leaflet produced by Britain's Liberal Democrats.

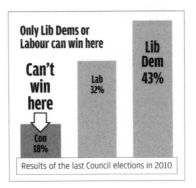

136

Opponents accuse the Lib Dems of dishonesty with images like this, but the graph is entirely factually accurate. There's no scale or axis, and the numbers are clearly displayed. Why not, indeed, go one step further, as Conservatives did in Dudley, near Birmingham, in 2014:

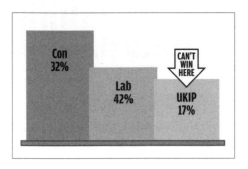

Now let's turn to what you decide to show. Let's say you're Apple, and you make what has been the world's most successful smartphone, the iPhone. After five years of phenomenal sales growth, they've slipped a bit, as competitors have caught up. They look, in fact, a little like the chart overleaf.

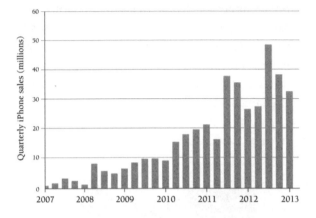

But you've got a big presentation of your new iPhone coming up, and you want to put a positive gloss on things. Wouldn't a chart like this be better?

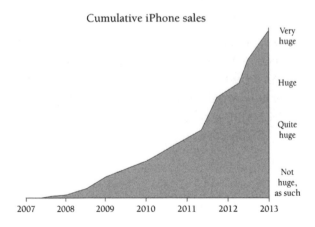

Cumulative iPhone sales

This is essentially the one that Apple CEO Tim Cook used in a September 2013 iPhone launch. (His didn't have any labels on the vertical axis at all, but he explained that sales of the iPhone were now 'very huge'. We've extrapolated the others.) It's a graph of total sales to date, and like everything produced by Apple it is, in its way, a thing of beauty. Using cumulative sales data means the line *can never go downwards*. If Apple only sold one iPhone in 2014, this graph would still show a tiny upward movement. If pressed to defend it, one could say that it's making a point about market penetration, except that this would assume that every iPhone ever sold was still in use.*

Let's see a cumulative figure combined with a percentage, for double the confusion (overleaf, top), produced by the British Labour Party. At first glance, it shows that not only are the energy companies sticking it to the ordinary man and woman, but they're sticking it to them by more every year. The problem faced by the graph's designers was that while the numbers definitely show energy bills rising well ahead of inflation each year, a bar chart of annual percentage increases looks like the next chart (overleaf, bottom).

---

*   The authors of this text may have been unaware of it, but the problems with Tim Cook's graph were first written up within hours of him showing it by David Yanofsky of the Quartz blog.

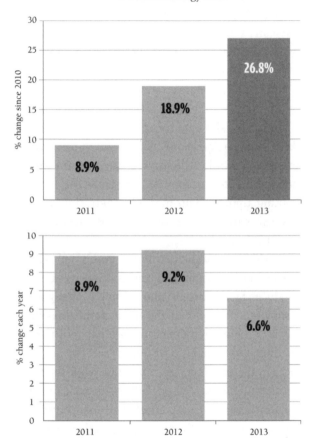

Domestic energy bills

Which makes it look vaguely like bills might actually be falling (they're not, but remember, no one understands percentages or inflation). Labour could have produced a graph of what's happening to annual bills that looked a bit like this:

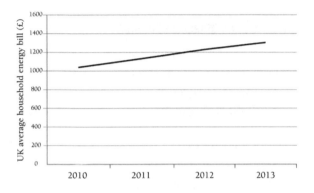

Or if that was felt to be undramatic, how about this:

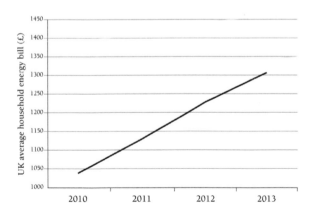

But of course, neither of those offered the dramatic increasing percentage that the cumulative total delivers.

Questions for group discussion

1. *When choosing between 'cash terms' and 'real terms' to illustrate a point, one should:*
   a) *discount for inflation*
   b) *choose the bigger one.*

2. *A good graph has:*
   a) *a clear, consistent scale*
   b) *a line that goes the way you want it to.*

FINAL NOTE

Here the text ends. As at the start of the book, final pages that might have given a clue as to the author's identity or intended audience were ripped out. I am no closer to guessing who they are, but I have started to become nervous about the extent of their reach. It seems ridiculous but when my laptop was stolen, as I was in the closing stages of preparing the manuscript for publication, I wondered if that was pure coincidence. I have concluded that if there is any threat to me, my greatest safety lies in publication. Perhaps the author, or authors, whoever they are, will put it about that this is simply a humorous work. But my publishers have promised me that the book will be sold as non-fiction contemporary history. And they're people of their word, I'm sure.

RH

ACKNOWLEDGEMENTS

I am, obviously, indebted both to the anonymous author of the text and its leaker. I will accept credit, but not blame, for their work.

Ben Bradlee's memoir about editing the *Washington Post*, quoted in A State of Undenial (see page 13), is *A Good Life*, published by Simon & Schuster. Tony Blair's *A Journey* is published by Arrow. J. K. Galbraith's *The Great Crash* is published by Houghton Mifflin Harcourt.

My editors at Elliott & Thompson, Jennie Condell and Pippa Crane, were of great assistance in preparing the text for publication.

In the course of researching and checking the accuracy of this text, I was assisted at various times, possibly without their knowledge, by Rafael Behr, Bonnie Brimstone, Peter Cavan, Matt Chorley, Torcuil Crichton, Sam Coates, Philip Cowley, Michael Deacon, Matthew Dearden, Stephen Dumughn, Damon Green, Helen Harden, Anna Hedge, Marcus and Ros Honeysett, Steve James, James Lyons, Sean Kemp, Gareth Milner, Jo Munday, Brian Nolan,

Matthew Parris, Jim Pickard, Hopi Sen, Andrew Sparrow, Ben Stanley, Bruno Vincent, Jim Waterson, Anthony Wells and Giles Wilkes.

My colleagues at Bloomberg News were patient with me as I searched through libraries of manuscripts around the world: Andrew Atkinson, Eddie Buckle, Alan Crawford, Kitty Donaldson, John Fraher, Reto Gregori, Reed V. Landberg, Svenja O'Donnell and Thomas Penny.

Finding myself with a book whose title was unknown, I described my problem to Iain Martin, who immediately suggested 'Would They Lie To You?'

My wife Sophie and my sons Fraser and Cameron were a source of constant interruptions, and I can only say that without them, the work would have been finished far sooner.